# BACKGROUND TO ENVIRONMENTAL PLANNING

# BACKGROUND TO
# ENVIRONMENTAL PLANNING

R. FRASER REEKIE
FRTPI, Dip.TP, FRIBA, Dip.Arch, FRSA
Principal Lecturer
Department of Town and Country Planning,
Bristol Polytechnic

Edward Arnold

© R. FRASER REEKIE 1975

First Published 1975
by Edward Arnold (Publishers) Ltd.
25 Hill Street, London W1X 8LL

Boards edition ISBN 0 7131 3341 4
Paper edition   ISBN 0 7131 3342 2

Filmset by Photoprint Plates Ltd., Rayleigh, Essex and
Printed in Great Britain by Fletcher & Son Ltd., Norwich

# Preface

The writing of this book was undertaken primarily to meet a need, expressed by teachers and others concerned with Town and Country Planning and its related fields of education and practice, for a concise general description of planning which would give an overall view of the subject and so provide a background to which detailed and specialised studies could be related.

The necessity is evinced by the unbalanced and distorted ideas that most new students and indeed most people have about planning. This may be a result of the biased propaganda of certain interests and the way planning matters are dealt with in newspapers and magazines, which tend to over-emphasise particular issues of the moment, and of the increasing complexity of planning.

Whatever the reason for the situation, the object of this book is to present a broad factual picture of planning in order to foster a greater awareness and a better understanding of what is involved.

Such a picture, imperfect though it may be, will be of value not only to students entering upon professional and technical courses in or connected with planning, but also to anyone who wishes to know more about the planning process. It can perhaps be of assistance in courses of environmental studies in secondary schools.

The book sets out firstly, to explain the basic meaning of planning and then, in sequence, to outline its historical development in Britain, to summarise present legislation, to describe planning practice, and to discuss some particular issues. A final chapter refers to education in planning. With so wide a scope there will be differences of opinion as to what should and what should not be included, but if the book achieves its main purpose it is hoped that any minor redundancies and omissions may be excused. It is not possible for a work like this to be up-to-date in every respect. Every day brings some change in national policies, in public attitudes, and in professional theories and methods. A new government, a new minister, a new situation can shift economic or social emphasis overnight. Nevertheless, the fundamentals of present-day planning will remain valid for a very long time.

I would like to thank all those who so willingly and kindly provided information and material, and who otherwise assisted in the preparation of this book, especially my colleague John Winter MA, Dip.TP, Cert.Ed, MRTPI, who read the draft and whose advice and comments were of great value.


R. FRASER REEKIE

# Contents

# 1
# The Idea of Planning

In the general sense of the word, planning is forward thinking or the making of advance arrangements, usually in the light of experience, for known or anticipated needs.

Simple examples of planning in everyday life are the drawing up of an itinerary for a projected journey with particulars of modes of travel, lengths of stays, time tables, etc., and the listing of things to be purchased perhaps with a statement of budgeted costs for each item prior to a shopping trip.

People, individually and collectively, have been planning since the beginnings of civilisation. Indeed, it is not too much to say that without planning there would be no civilisation; man would have remained an animal behaving according to instinct and reacting only to the immediate situation. There would be no social or political organisation except of the crudest kind, no agriculture, no crafts or manufactures, no building and certainly no arts. The idea of planning and, in consequence, the exercise of control in accordance with planned intention are fundamental to most human activities.

And yet, until comparatively recent times, the concept of planning was not applied or was applied only to a limited extent in regard to what has become a matter of the greatest importance, affecting the lives of everyone, and upon which the progress of the world towards increased efficiency and happiness more and more depends. This is the utilisation of land and resources, the design and construction of buildings and communications, and the concomitant shaping of interacting social and economic policies. This kind of planning has been and still is described as 'Town and Country Planning' or 'Urban and Regional Planning', but neither of these terms fully conveys the

1

meaning of the present day concept. It is better explained by the expression 'Environmental Planning', thus indicating its wider scope in including the whole of our natural and man-made surroundings.

The following chapter, in outlining the historical background, traces planning in this modern sense. It started in the early nineteenth century when in Britain and elsewhere minds were turned to ways of solving the problems resulting from the concentrations of a rapidly increasing population in overcrowded, insanitary and ugly towns, and the despoilation of large areas of the countryside by industrial plant, sprawling factories and extensive mineral workings.

From the efforts of philanthropic mill-owners to ameliorate the living and labouring conditions of their workers by, amongst other things, the provision of a better standard of dwellings and amenities, and the schemes for 'ideal' cities imagined by utopian visionaries, through the more direct and widespread action of Government to improve urban housing and so eradicate or reduce epidemic diseases by such legislation as Public Health Acts and Building Bye-laws, to the proposals of social reformers and garden city promoters, the idea of planned and controlled development of land and buildings as a means of furthering the physical and mental well-being of people as a whole became generally accepted.

The early nineteen-hundreds saw the embodiment of town planning ideas in specific legislation, and there followed during the first half of the twentieth century a succession of acts and related laws expanding their range and application culminating in the wide-reaching Act of 1947. Development planning and control was exercised by departments of designated local authorities, and much good work was done in the fields of housing and slum clearance, in the preservation of amenities, in the redevelopment of town centres, and in the building of new towns. But some ten years ago it became apparent that patterns of thought and action had fallen behind the needs of a rapidly changing world. Official planning was too rigidly determinate for the long term, yet development plans were not sufficiently detailed for those areas where early implementation was called for. Criticisms that the planning system was inadequate were accompanied by doubts about its aims. Former principles and theories were re-examined. Concurrently, new prediction and design techniques and methodologies, derived in part from military and commercial uses, were introduced. There was a wide-spread awareness of the inter-relationships between physical planning, which had received undue emphasis in the past, and all other kinds of planning, especially social and economic, affecting the total environment.

There was a growing realisation that, because of increasing populations, rising standards of living and increased leisure combined with greater mobility, there would soon be a limit to many of the natural resources upon which present day living depends and which had previously been taken for granted; also, because of the increased volume of wastes produced, the environment is not only being polluted but is in danger of being destroyed.

This ferment of new ideas brought about considerable changes in legislation, practice and education. New acts and regulations, now current, provide for a new approach to planning strategy and tactics, and for greater public participation in the planning process. Practice makes use of more sophisticated techniques and has become a highly complex team-work effort of interlocking specialisms. Necessarily, there have been concomitant changes in professional attitudes and in planning education. There has also been a reorganisation of local government, in which new ideas about management and corporate planning – the integration of the objectives of all departments – are being put into effect.

These far-reaching innovations, which are referred to in more detail in later pages, are now being put into practice, and for some years, further major changes in legislation and practice are unlikely. There will of course be new ideas and new theories propounded from time to time. If shown to be valid, they will increase the efficiency of planning and will facilitate the realisation of its aims. But the world does not stand still, and many problems are too urgent to wait for solutions that depend upon the testing of untried suppositions or political manoeuvering. Many important planning decisions must continue to be made professionally on a basis of available knowledge, skills and reasonable assumptions – which will be more accurately assessed as 'tools' are refined and experience grows – within acceptable social limits and practical and economic constraints of existing circumstances.

# 2
# Historical Outline

All history is fascinating, and the history of planning as one aspect of human progress is particularly interesting in its relationship to political, economic and social thought. But it is not only of value as a subject in its own right, but also of particular practical value, because in Britain so many layouts, buildings and structures of the past still exist. They cannot be ignored and present-day planning has to take them into account. Therefore, the better they are understood in their historical context the better their worth can be assessed. If of sufficient age or merit, they are protected, either singly or in groups, by legislation (see Chapter 3), and the practice of planning is very much concerned with the carrying out of this obligation, as it is part of the preservation of the Nation's cultural heritage.

The subject of planning history is, of course, a vast one, and there are many books which deal with it. Here, it is only possible to indicate a thread, as it were, with special reference to Britain. Accordingly, the early settlements of prehistoric peoples and of the ancient world must be passed over, and a start made with the Classical Greek period when some new towns were systematically planned on a simple grid pattern of roads giving convenient rectangular sites for buildings, and with certain plots designated for important public uses such as temples, theatres, stadium and agora; the last-named being a more or less centrally located open air meeting place for free citizens.

However, it was the Romans who first established planned towns on a considerable scale. Although Rome itself grew haphazardly and suffered from many of the problems that beset cities of later times — overcrowding, narrow and inadequate streets, insanitary and unhealthy residential quarters — elsewhere, with characteristic order and

4

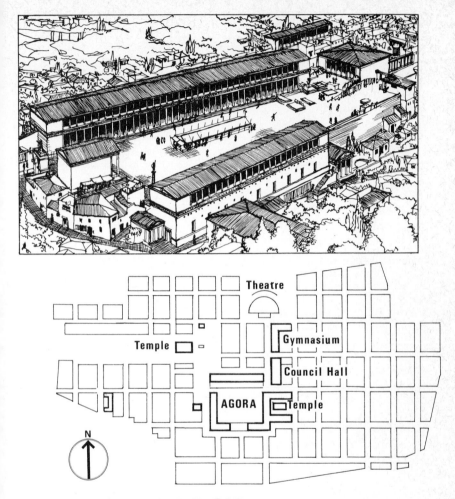

# PRIENE GREEK CITY

CLASSICAL GREEK TOWNS   Lower drawing shows a simplified plan of
Priene, a typical third century BC city, laid out with a characteristic rectangular
grid system of roads — limited in this instance by an edge of rocky outcrop
on which the settlement is situated, and with a centrally located agora and
public buildings.
Perspective, above, is a reconstruction of the agora at Assos. The Agora
was the focal point of Greek cities, a general meeting place for all purposes —
political, religious, commercial and recreation — for the privileged section
of the community. *(reproduced from 'World Architecture' by permission of
the Hamlyn Group Picture Library).*

regularity, the Romans founded well laid-out towns throughout the territories of their empire. The standard pattern was based on the crossing of two main streets leading to gates in the defensive walls of a rectangular area. At the crossing of the streets, that is, at the centre of the town, was the forum, a rectangular open space corresponding to the Greek agora and similarly surrounded by public buildings and adorned with statues and such-like features. Vehicles were not normally allowed to enter the forum, access to which was by footways from the remainder of the settlement. The public buildings usually included a basilica or meeting hall, temples, administrative offices and, in the larger towns, the thermae, a combination of baths and other social facilities, and perhaps a theatre.

The rest of the area was divided into rectangular sites for dwellings of various kinds and possibly military barracks. The basic plan is in fact that of a typical military camp, from which it was doubtless derived.

## Roman Britain

There are many examples of Roman towns and camps in Britain, and it was the Romans who first brought physical planning to this country. The influence of their layouts is still to be traced in those towns which began as Roman settlements. However, the Romans did much more than introduce planned towns. The location of their settlements established regional centres and markets connected by a network of roads for rapid communication. They cleared forests and promoted agriculture, thus changing the face of the countryside. By maintaining peace and order over most of the island, they made possible the rise of civilised life. This may indeed have been autocratic rule, obnoxious in some respects, but preferable to the barbarism, terror and complete negation of planning which followed the withdrawal of Roman forces and the onset of the 'Dark Ages'.

## Medieval Britain

It was not until the Norman Conquest that again a strong central government brought order and stability to most parts of the country and so produced conditions for the growth of permanent settlements. During the Middle Ages the political and economic systems were feudal, but considerable power was also exercised by the Church. Villages developed, some later becoming towns, outside the walls of castles or near monastic or other ecclesiastical foundations.

Medieval urban areas were of two categories. The majority were not planned. They grew 'naturally' as needs arose, commonly in a concentric fashion or somewhat star-shaped as later structures spread out along radial approach roads, but modified according to topographical conditions. This type of development is known as *adaptive*. But there was also a minority of planned towns, located on deliberately selected sites with a regular layout of streets on the grid pattern, with pre-determined positions for principal public buildings. This was the obvious arrangement for producing convenient rectangular plots and the design used basically for new towns and even for the subdivision of land, until increased vehicular traffic made crossroads dangerous. Overall size was often defined by a defensive wall. Such towns were constructed for purposes of controlling territories or to attract settlers, sometimes to lure them away from older trading centres, in order to

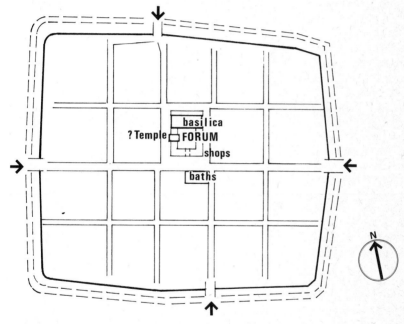

## CAERWENT ROMAN CITY

CLASSICAL ROMAN TOWNS    Simplified plan of a Roman provincial settlement in Britain at Caerwent, Wales, showing a typical rectangular area enclosed by defensive walls and, in this case, ditches, with grid layout of roads. The arrangement is unusual in that the north and south gates are not exactly opposite one another owing to the uneven number of east-west divisions. Centrally located is the Forum with basilica and various public buildings around it.

promote commerce. These medieval planned towns are known as 'bastides'* and a few were founded in England and Wales by King Edward I. One of the best known is Winchelsea, but not all survived and they had little influence on later developments.

Characteristic of the medieval towns in general is that, apart from an irregular market place, the central area was crowded with tightly-packed buildings whose continuous frontages lined narrow, winding lanes — the routes of animals and walking man. Standards of construction, except for churches and important public buildings, was poor. Water supply and drainage was primitive and the lack of hygiene resulted in frequent outbreaks of serious diseases. The closeness of the buildings, most of which were largely of timber, increased the likelihood and rapid spread of devastating fires.

Market places were often large to accommodate cattle and sheep pens as well as produce stalls. Many still exist, although sometimes encroached upon in later years. The market place was the focal point of the community, a reflection but an unplanned one of the Greek agora and the Roman forum, and around it were the parish church, town hall, hostelries, ale houses and the like. But it differed from its classical forerunners in being open to all. It was devoted primarily to trade, mainly the produce of agriculture, farming and associated crafts. Rural settlements of the same period were less crowded and usually consisted of a loose assembly of buildings around a green or strung out along a highway. The persistence of the latter arrangement to the present day aggravates the danger and damage from heavy goods vehicles passing through villages and will do so until alternative routes are provided.

Few medieval towns and villages have escaped transformation, most having been largely rebuilt in succeeding centuries, but their layouts set the patterns for later roads with resulting problems of central area congestion. Those that have remained intact often exhibit great charm. This is not because they were unplanned and the majority of the buildings not consciously designed, for non-planning and non-design is not a prescription for an attractive built environment but, because they were constructed necessarily of common local materials within tight limitations of techniques and skills for relatively simple uses; there is a unity of colour, texture, scale and architectural detail which, fortuitously in these instances, exists in a visually satisfying cohesiveness that has been enhanced by years of weathering, and the whole effect is further heightened by the presence of mature trees, natural growth and perhaps a picturesque landscape setting. Whether or not this charm can be achieved intentionally in prevailing conditions

* from the French 'batir', to build

MEDIEVAL VILLAGE   Mixed vernacular buildings of local materials, stone, timber and plaster, at medieval village of Lacock, Wiltshire, fortuitously impart an atmosphere of romantic charm. *(photo: courtesy of National Trust)*

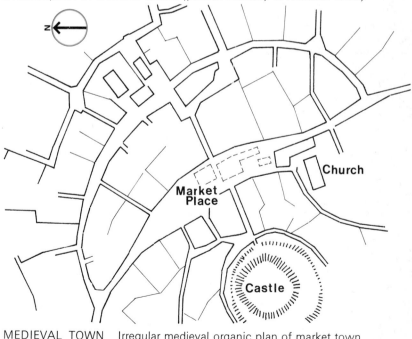

MEDIEVAL TOWN   Irregular medieval organic plan of market town developed outwards from settlement at approach to Norman castle. The broken lines indicate later encroachments on the market place around which were main hostelries and public buildings.

is doubtful; efforts to do so may lead to spurious copies having at best only a superficial and transitory attractiveness.

## The Renaissance in Britain

The great movement known as the Renaissance, a supposed re-birth of the ideas and forms of classical art, began in the fourteenth century in Italian states. It coincided with the decline of the feudal, monastic and agrarian systems and the rise of an urban mercantile commercial civilisation; a shift of power from state and church to merchants and capitalists. It spread to Britain in the fifteenth century and became generally accepted in the sixteenth century. It is difficult to summarise briefly the enormous effects on every aspect of life, but some that were of importance to planning were: the emergence of architects and town planners in the sense of specialists in physical design, a leap forward in construction techniques, organisation and skills, a marked increase in the use of horses for riding and the drawing of vehicles with a consequent need for better roads, and an emphasis on sym-metrical and geometrical layouts and building design, together with formal gardens often of considerable extent.

Ideas in architecture and town planning were first imported, into England by way of Holland, but later they came from direct contact with Italy, as exemplified by the works of Inigo Jones (the tercentenary of whose death was commemorated in 1973) and of Sir Christopher Wren. The latter's plan for London after the Great Fire of 1666, which destroyed much of the old medieval city, was based on Italian and French renaissance models. The plan was not carried out, and unlike some continental countries Britain did not see the Renaissance ex-pressed in the building of new towns on previously undeveloped sites or by large-scale extensions to existing towns, but rather in piecemeal additions on fields and gardens and by the replacement of medieval slums.

However, towards the end of the eighteenth century Britain's great and increasing prosperity to the benefit of the upper and rising middle classes resulted in considerable and mostly speculative residen-tial building schemes in major cities and spas and, incidentally, the giving of 'face-lifts' in the new style to old medieval structures. It is from this period that the much admired Georgian terraces and 'squares' originated. This architecture still gives a special character and is a dominant influence in many towns. The better examples are considered eminently worthy of preservation and conservation (see p. 117). Nevertheless, these fine buildings and the associated dignified and graceful layouts of roads and open space were for the wealthy, although many have since fallen in the social scale. The poorer section of the population continued to live in crowded and often squalid conditions, so that socially the separation of classes was emphasised.

In the Regency period that followed, large scale urban developments in an even grander manner continued.

In rural areas, changes occurred in the countryside during the eighteenth century owing to the introduction of new methods of agriculture which tended to increase the size of farming units. Thousands of enclosure acts from 1761 to 1844 resulted in the typical English scene of relatively large fields bounded by hedges and hedgerow trees — now disappearing in eastern parts where modern ways of farming by mechanical means require greater areas of cleared land. While the enclosures made farming more efficient they brought about the extinction of yeoman freeholders and transformed villagers into landless labourers.

Other changes were wrought by 'landscape gardeners', the fore-runners of landscape architects, who obliterated the formal garden layouts of the early renaissance and in their place created great parks in the 'natural' manner for the big landowners of the time. Many trees were planted, artificial lakes were made and 'features' such as temples, bridges and cottages were introduced. Conversely, anything considered discordant was removed, even to the extent of resiting a whole village!

## Nineteenth-century Britain

The agricultural changes and mechanical inventions of the latter part of the preceding century exploded into the industrial revolution of the nineteenth century when steam power-driven machinery and transport caused an upheavel in the economic and social life of the nation. The story of this transformation has been recounted many times and can be found in detail elsewhere. Only the main effects which, as stated previously, brought about the real beginning of institutional town planning can be touched upon here. Socially, the gulf between the wealthy and the poor widened. Dispossessed agricultural labourers and former self-employed spinners and weavers, the country cottage dwellers, became the collective, impersonalised, minimum-wage 'hands' in factories and mills, or the workers in pits and mines, compelled to live where they could find employment.

The first factories were located near sources of coal and iron — energy and raw material — with reasonable access to roads and waterways, but the coming of railways provided faster and better means of transport and made possible greater flexibility of situation. Towns with industries

expanded enormously as they attracted more and more people to serve more and more machines producing more and more manufactured goods for home and overseas markets. But the housing of those people was left to a new kind of speculative builder whose sole concern was, not surprisingly, to cram as many dwellings into as little space as possible, although in mitigation of their action it should be realised that they had to build cheaply so that the workers could afford to pay the necessary low rent from their meagre pay. In some respects, the accommodation may not have been much worse than that of the hovels of villages and hamlets of the day, but there were no compensations of open space, gardens, fresh air and sunlight. On the contrary, crowded into confined rows of back-to-back houses without through ventilation or adequate sanitary facilities in the shadow and murk of grim factories or down in pits, spending long hours of hard work in appalling conditions of noise, smells, semi-darkness and danger, it is no wonder that the lives of the workers was for the most part brutish and short, and that diseases spread like wildfire.

One cause of congestion in towns was that until the mid-eighteen-eighties and beyond a majority of workers had to walk to their jobs and therefore had to live close to their places of employment. But later, improved roads made possible the use of horse-drawn private transport and omnibuses, and by 1860 tramways and metropolitan and suburban railways promoted the outward spread of residential areas at least for managerial and clerical staffs. However, this improvement in passenger transport brought increased traffic into the central areas and thus began a problem which has still to be solved satisfactorily.

Railways exacerbated industrial pollution of the urban environment by adding to the smoke, fumes, noise and dirt, and complicated redevelopment of built-up areas by taking large areas of land for stations, goods yards, and tracks and by making unrelated divisions and barriers between different parts of every town they entered.

As the better-off middle classes moved out to suburban areas in houses at four to eight to the acre or, if not so well off to rows of 'villas' and 'semis'. so their former dwellings, late Georgian and Regency terraces, were divided into tenements for multi-occupancy by the poor. This segregation by districts hastened the breakdown of community life, such that remained, and hardened the separate class structure. There was general unconcern by those above for the plight of the less

EIGHTEENTH-CENTURY RENAISSANCE ARCHITECTURE AND FORMAL PLANNING IN BRITAIN   Aerial view of layout of houses for the noble and the wealthy in the grand manner: the Circus, the Royal Crescent, and the connecting terraces of Georgian Bath Spa, a city on the site of the former Roman settlement of Aqua Sulis. *(photo: West Air Photography)*

fortunate, and Government was slow to act to improve working and living conditions of the 'lower classes', notwithstanding isolated efforts of some writers and public figures to draw attention to the plight of the masses existing in the degrading and disgusting slums of London and the major industrial towns.

However, a number of idealist reformers did contribute to the slowly evolving idea of planning in the modern sense. Their work had considerable influence later in the century. One of the first of these pioneers of progress was Robert Owen, whose practical approach in showing that successful factories could be operated outside towns in salubrious surrounding together with good housing and amenities for the workers, and his contention that land use could be controlled in the interests of the community as a whole inspired others. There followed a succession of schemes for ideal settlements, and some industrialists actually built 'model villages' for their employees with emphasis on well-spaced homes and gardens. Late nineteenth-century examples of such limited planning are Bourneville and Port Sunlight.

From the concept of garden-villages for the welfare of workers in a particular factory, grew the idea of designing complete new towns providing for varied employment, a balanced society, residences of all kinds and recreational and cultural facilities — an idea coming pretty close to that on which present-day New Towns are based. But the plans suffered from excessive formality and symmetry of layout and the peculiar architectural styles of the period. And there was always the difficulty of financing such schemes. J. S. Buckingham's *Victoria* is an example of this kind of unrealised and unrealisable project.

But the good intentions of a few well-meaning industrialists and visionaries, while paving the way for subsequent planning, made little

MILTON ABBAS, DORSET, a late eighteenth-century village designed by landscape-architect 'Capability' Brown for the Earl of Dorchester, who wished to remove the insalubrious medieval 'town' of Milton from close to his mansion. Some inhabitants were bought out; others forcibly evicted by flooding! Perhaps this is the first fully-planned village in England, the lay-out exhibits many present-day ideas. Although the village is linear, a serpentine road following an inclined valley slope with strategically placed larger buildings provides changing perspectives and adds interest to the rows of cob-walled, thatched-roofed cottages. Landscaping was integrated with buildings, and originally chestnut trees were planted between dwellings, which have open front lawns and private rear gardens.
Intended primarily to house the dispossessed humble country folk, the cottages are now almost all modernised internally and occupied by relatively affluent professional and upper middle-class 'retired' and 'week-enders' — see p. 109.

Photograph shows a view of the village from the church tower looking West. *(Jarrold and Sons Limited)*

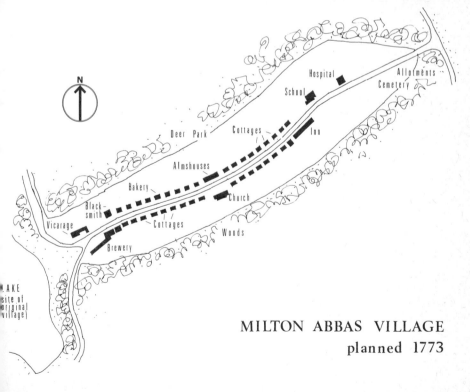

N

Deer Park

Cottages

Hospital

School

Allotments
Cemetery

Inn

Almshouses

Bakery

Church

Black-
smith

Vicarage

Cottages

Brewery

Woods

LAKE
(site of
original
village)

MILTON ABBAS VILLAGE
planned 1773

impression in their own time and were of no avail against the un-controlled growth of the great majority of towns which were expanding rapidly to accommodate the equally uncontrolled increase in population and the proliferation of industry. There was no real advance in over-coming the congestion and chaos of the urban conditions and the horrible housing of lower-paid workers until Government was made aware at last of the causes of epidemic diseases such as cholera, and began to legislate against the worst evils. An important milestone was the great Public Health Act of 1875, which laid upon local authorities the duty of enforcing sanitary codes and building by-laws governing town growth. This may be regarded as the start of planning law. Most authorities adopted by-laws that specified minimum standards for roads and for the construction of buildings, including open space about them for through ventilation, sanitary facilities, etc., and also provided for the closing of houses unfit for habitation. Admirable though these measures were in relation to what had gone before, speculative builders, while complying with the letter of the requirements, did so at least cost by putting up long rows of straight parallel streets of dreary monotonous brick-walled, slate-roofed houses with an almost total lack of visual amenity. Miles of 'By-law Housing' still remain in many towns. Much has been done in recent years to improve such areas and, in present circumstances, to bring them up to acceptable standards is an important planning activity.

Where public and commercial buildings were concerned, the latter part of the nineteenth century saw something of a rebirth of civic pride which, if it did little to resolve the now gigantic urban problems of chaotic development in central areas where factories, coal-gas works, houses, offices, churches, etc., were all jumbled together in an unholy mess, and the streets, often jammed with vehicles of various kinds, did

EARLY NINETEENTH-CENTURY ROADS   Unplanned meandering roads wandering northwards from Bristol town limits; compare with present-day aerial photograph and map of much the same area on pp. 22–23.
Redland, at top of this map, contained some private houses including Redland Court – see p. 68. Many of them still exist but are put to other uses and engulfed by Victorian terraces, which in turn are giving way to blocks of flats and offices.
Of the extensive nursery gardens indicated towards the left of the map, it is interesting to note that nearly 150 years later, one small area remains as a 'Garden Centre'.
Eighteenth-century Kingsdown, bottom right, was largely destroyed during the Second World War and has been redeveloped as a residential estate of flats and 'partio' or courtyard houses which show as a checkerboard pattern on the above-mentioned aerial map.
*(part of plan of Bristol by B. Donne 1826 reproduced by kind permission of Bristol City Museum)*

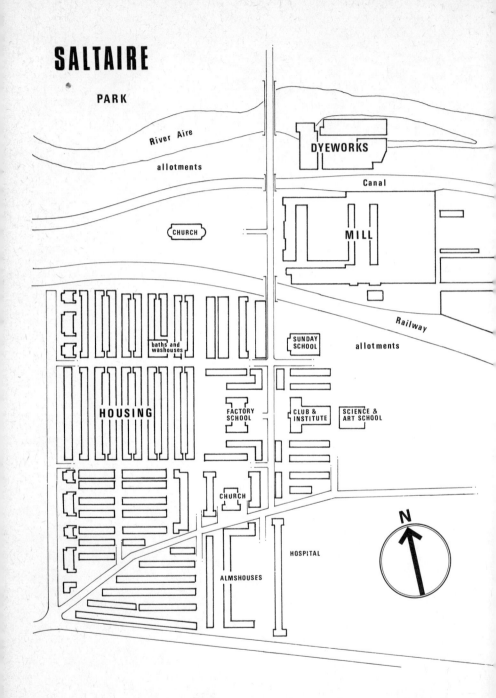

# SALTAIRE

PARK

River Aire

allotments

DYEWORKS

Canal

CHURCH

MILL

Railway

allotments

baths and
washouses

SUNDAY
SCHOOL

HOUSING

FACTORY
SCHOOL

CLUB &
INSTITUTE

SCIENCE &
ART SCHOOL

CHURCH

HOSPITAL

N

ALMSHOUSES

## NINETEENTH-CENTURY 'MODEL VILLAGE' OF SALTAIRE, YORKSHIRE

One of the earliest examples of a planned industrial village built between 1850 and 1871 by philanthropist mill-owner, Sir Titus Salt, to improve the living conditions of his workers. Although a 'company' settlement, it had all the elements of a complete town — see plan opposite — including housing of various kinds, schools, churches, hospital, almshouses, public baths and facilities for leisure and recreation (but no 'pub'!). Communications were well provided by roads, railway, river and canal.

The photograph above shows a typical terrace. Although the general appearance may not seem very different from contemporary housing, much greater care was taken in regard to architectural and constructional design. The dwellings were much in advance of the usual standard of their day. All had through ventilation and were well equipped internally. Designing was preceded by what would now be called a social survey to ascertain people's needs. The photograph to the right is of the statue of Sir Titus Salt which stands in the park he gave to the people. *(photos: John Watson)*

produce individual buildings of extraordinary eclectic architectural styles. The wealth of the British Empire plus that of industrial prosperity enabled municipal councils and leading local worthies to erect exuberant edifices — town halls, museums and art galleries, and the like — and the business communities to construct their head offices, banks and hotels in corresponding florid fashion. Many of these monumental works remain. Some have outlived their original purpose or are no longer economical; they pose questions of preservation and alternative utilisation.

By the end of the century, electricity for lighting and motive power, the internal combustion engine for road transport, and oil (petroleum) as a major source of energy were heralding a new technological era. Great social changes were also taking place: political socialism, trade unionism, the emancipation of women, improved care and education of children, a better understanding of requirements for health were but a few of the contributory factors radically to alter ways of living. The idea of planning took a leap forward by the publication in 1898 of *Tomorrow,* later called *Garden Cities of Tomorrow,* written by Ebenezer Howard, in which he advocated the building of a defined compact town about one and a half miles in diameter set in the middle of an agricultural area — a green belt. The town, which he illustrated diagrammatically, was to be based on industry and commerce (employment), and would contain a balanced mixture of social groups (social integration). All houses would have gardens and would be within easy reach of factories, shops, schools, and the open country. At the heart of the town would be a central park around which would be public buildings and places of entertainment. Factories were to be located on the periphery served by an encircling railway, which would not enter the town, but would have radial connections to surrounding 'satellite' towns beyond the 'green belt'. It was fundamental to the concept that when the prescribed urban area was fully developed, new towns beyond the agricultural reservation should be started. The proposal received considerable support in principle and ultimately led to the founding of Letchworth Garden City and Welwyn Garden City within the next twenty-five years.

The comparatively unspoiled rural landscape of the eighteenth century was sorely affected by the industrial revolution. Mines and pits, slag heaps, mineral workings, brickfields and a multitude of factories and mean houses spread like some manifestation of plague over much of the land, and the countryside was scored, gashed and piled upon by railway lines, cuttings and embankments. The noble landowners of great estates and their large-scale landscapers were succeeded by an increasing number of new rich industrialists and merchants whose

NINETEENTH-CENTURY INDUSTRIAL TOWNS    Illustrations of typical rows of crowded dreary 'back-to-back' and 'bye-law' houses in central areas, with inadequate sunlight, ventilation and open spaces.
Upper picture from television 'Coronation Street' *(courtesy — Granada Television Limited)*
Lower picture shows older part of Leeds *(reproduced by permission of Director of Planning, Leeds City Council)*

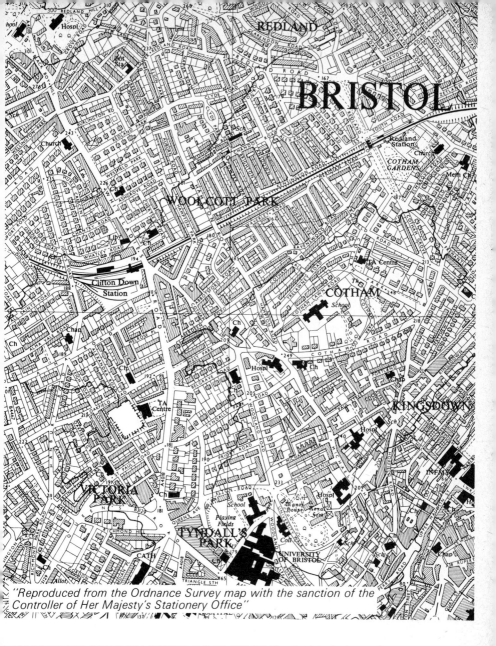

NINETEENTH-CENTURY TOWN DEVELOPMENT   Aerial photograph, facing page, of part of Bristol in the County of Avon and, above, the corresponding area as shown on Ordnance Survey map no. ST 57 SE (for detail see map on p. 68). The main roads in many instances follow the lines of meandering roads and lanes that led out of the town in former times when most of the land was open country (see map on p. 17). The buildings include some isolated eighteenth-century houses, but the majority of the development took place in the Victorian era. The mid nineteenth-century railway track skirted the periphery of the then built-up area and so promoted the further outward spread of residences. (photo: West Air Photography)

EBENEZER HOWARD    Photograph of memorial plaque to Ebenezer Howard
at a focal point in the avenue layout of Welwyn New Town, Herts. The
lettering reads: 'Sir Ebenezer Howard 1850–1928. Founder of Welwyn
Garden City in 1920. His vision and practical idealism profoundly affected
town planning throughout the world'.
On the opposite page are simplified diagrams of (bottom) Howard's Garden
City, and (top) his concept of a 'group of slumless smokeless cities', i.e. new
towns disposed about a fully developed urban area with intervening
'green belts'.

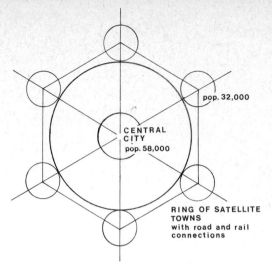

## DIAGRAM OF GROUP OF TOWNS

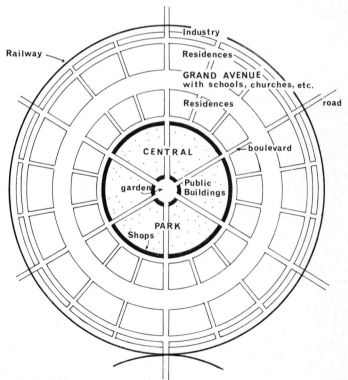

## CENTRAL GARDEN CITY

smaller domains were cultivated by gardeners of a different type, in stylistic fashions as varied as the architecture of contemporary buildings. Some layouts were informal in a too obviously contrived manner, others were fussily geometric to an absurd degree. The baleful influence of these extremes are still to be seen in miniature in some private and public gardens of today. But on the credit side, interest in tree planting of unusual kinds imported from the colonies and in the growing of exotic plants, shrubs and grasses fostered a love of nature and the pleasures of the open air that was to find expression in the establishing of municipal parks and recreation grounds.

## Twentieth-century Britain

Despite the spread of the idea of planning amongst thinking people there was at first little change to improve urban conditions in the twentieth century. The poorer members of the population were still housed in decaying central districts or in dreary by-law terraces or, in some towns, in warren-like tenements, all equally lacking in amenities. Other classes lived in more or less concentric belts of diminishing densities and improving quality the more distant they were from the centre. Building remained in private hands although it was becoming recognised that housing for the working classes might well have to be a matter for direct Government action.

Certainly, there were influential advocates of the desirability of considering towns as a whole and of making studies of town design and of the need to control by legal means all building development and land use. Others, in a restricted field, were earnestly pressing for measures to relieve congestion in town centres and to restore (?) the art of civic design, the creation of dignified buildings in spacious surroundings. Some espoused the case for preserving historic buildings. These campaigns in regard to fundamentals of urban planning led to the first specific planning legislation in Britain: the Housing, Town Planning, etc. (*sic*) Act of 1909, which empowered but did not compel local authorities to prepare town planning schemes with the object of securing proper sanitary conditions, amenity and convenience in connection with the laying out and use of land. It did not apply to built-up land or non-urban land and so, in effect, merely regulated new suburban developments. However, a start had been made and it was to be followed by a succession of Planning Acts and related legislation during the next sixty years.

The First World War interrupted progress and the post-war situation brought about an unprecedented boom in building, especially housing. Notwithstanding the good intentions of further legislation and the

WELWYN GARDEN CITY   Founded by private enterprise in 1920 and subsequently taken over under the New Towns Act 1946 — see p. 77 — Welwyn Garden City shows in the tradition-based design of its buildings, formal layout and careful integration of landscape and street furniture, a maturity and dignity that sets it apart from later New Towns. These pictures, reproduced with the permission of the Commission of the New Towns, are two views of the Town Centre.

example set by the founding of Howard's second garden city at Welwyn, developments spread rapidly outwards from existing towns into random suburban estates wherever land was obtainable, and along highways (ribbon development). Schemes took no regard of basic planning principles, and were pushed along by market demand and availability of cheap travel by railways, buses and private cars. The liberal provision of construction advances as well as purchase loans by Building Societies gave a great stimulus to speculative builders of houses for lower middle and middle income groups.

Light industries also spread to the suburbs but locations took no account of relating workers' housing, so for many people long costly journeys became necessary thus causing unnecessary traffic. The sprawl of industry was particularly manifest in the South-East and the Midlands.

Housing for the so-called working classes now passed entirely into the hands of local authorities as private enterprise could no longer produce dwelling to be let at rents which this section of the community could afford. Enormous subsidised 'council estates' were built consisting mainly of short terraces or semi-detached houses. Although standards of accommodation were reasonably good, layouts were formal and geometric (drawing board designs), and little provision was made for social facilities such as local shopping centres, schools and community buildings, or for public open spaces and recreation areas. Physical segregation of classes was continued. The idea of planned towns for a balanced community suffered a set-back.

The 'depression' (economic slump) of the late nineteen-twenties and early nineteen-thirties resulted in widespread unemployment and consequent distress amongst the 'working' population, especially in areas with one already declining industry. There was a drift to the less badly hit South-East and the Midlands. This situation led to another significant intervention by Government in respect to the location of industry. Trading estates, i.e. planned factory areas, were set up in depressed areas to provide a variety of employment. These were a precedent for later 'industrial estates', a now accepted element of town plans, and for other Government measures to direct and influence the location of industry. Development in general slowed down to some extent, but private house building continued unchecked in the thirties until the shadow of the coming conflict cast a blight over the country.

The Second World War again stopped all but essential building. Aerial bombardment destroyed great areas of many cities. War damage caused the loss of thousands of homes, and many central areas were wiped out. That this would provide an opportunity for replanning and rebuilding along new lines was foreseen by the Government. The

Barlow Report[1] was published in 1940 and the Scott Report[2] and the Uthwatt Report[3] in 1942. Other reports bearing on the subject were published during and shortly after the war. It was the intention of Government, reflecting now widely-held views, to secure better use of the land and resources of the country. Various laws were enacted. Of major importance was the Town and Country Planning Act of 1947, which made a fresh start by repealing all previous planning legislation and which brought the development or redevelopment of almost all land under planning control. Other acts followed, but the next big advance was the Town and Country Planning Act of 1968, amended by the Town and Country Planning Act, 1971, now the basic Act, and the Town and Country Planning (Amendment) Act of 1972, and this is the basis of current planning law which is dealt with in the following chapter. Earlier Acts relating to particular aspects of planning are incorporated, including Control of Office and Industrial Development Act of 1966 and the Civic Amenities Act of 1967.

It can be said that the last twenty-five years has been a period of considerable progress in planning attitudes, legislation and techniques, and one of increasing Government involvement.

The New Towns Act of 1946 provided for balanced residential, industrial and commercial developments, and the Town Development Act of 1951 provided for the planned expansion of existing towns on similar lines. Much has been achieved (see Chapter 5).

New residential areas are now designed in conjunction with appropriate shops, schools, community buildings and with adequate public open spaces for amenity, play and games. Shopping centres are laid out as traffic-free precincts reached by convenient footpaths and public transport. Various types of out-of-town and out-of-centre retailing facilities, primarily for car-borne shoppers, have appeared. National and country parks reserved for recreation and leisure use, and areas of outstanding beauty are protected against unsightly developments.

Road communications have been improved and a network of high-speed motorways is extending across the country

Apart from physical achievements, more important, perhaps, is the fact that town and country planning has become generally accepted

[1] dealt with causes of distribution of industrial population, future tendencies, social, economic and strategic disadvantages of concentration, remedial measures

[2] considered conditions which should govern developments in country areas consistent with maintenance of agriculture, factors affecting location of industry, the well-being of rural communities and preservation of rural amenities

[3] dealt with problems of compensation and betterment; stressed need for central planning authority

by public opinion as in the interests of the community as a whole, accompanied though it must be by a curtailment of a degree of the freedom of the individual and conflict with the profit objectives of private developers.

There are compelling reasons for concerted planning in its widest sense at international level, e.g. the effects of Britain's entry into the European Economic Community, the construction of the Channel Tunnel, certain kinds of pollution, and the energy crisis; at national level for domestic repercussions of the foregoing and to implement major policy decisions of the Central Government; and at regional and local levels, where there are still many problems. The inherited mistakes of the past, the decaying and dilapidated urban areas, derelict industrial areas, the continued mis-use and squandering of natural resources, the pollution and poisoning of the environment by inefficient disposal of wastes, inorganic refuse and effluents, and by excessive noise and visual clutter, traffic congestion, the spread of residential development, now eating into the once inviolate 'green belts' under pressure of a dangerously increasing population, the ever-present threat to fine old buildings and natural landscape from the greed of unscrupulous exploiters, are all problems that need to be solved.

So to the present day — a time of rapid change in a politically and economically unstable world, but never before so great an awareness of the consequence of human actions. The record of accomplishments resulting from the constantly evolving process of planning provides some encouragement that progress can continue towards the achievement of a good environment and a just and fair life for all.

# 3
# Planning Legislation

Planning can be carried out without formal laws. An all-powerful potentate or for that matter a community of like-minded virtuous men and women can theoretically 'plan' a more or less self-sustaining territory — utilise resources, determine the uses of land, lay out communications, select sites for buildings; in short, can order all things that constitute a man-made environment without elaborate legislative machinery. Smaller areas of land in one private ownership can be planned physically in the same way.

But in practice and particularly in a large industrialised developed country with a long history, inhabited by a society in which personal acquisitiveness and competition and downright greed are far from absent, laws are necessary to ensure that certain things are done and other things are not done according to what is believed to be in the common interest. A government which, hopefully, represents in a so-called democratic system, the wishes of the majority, formulates and enforces the laws.

From the previous chapter it can be seen that in Britain, laws relating to planning were initially passed to deal with unhealthy and otherwise undesirable conditions resulting from the industrial revolution. Gradually, legislation was extended by successive Acts: there now exists a considerable body of law covering the whole country and virtually every kind of physical development, redevelopment and land use, affecting everyone in some way or another. It is doubtful if there is any other branch of law so extensive in its application.

No attempt is made here to summarise town and country planning law and related legislation, but merely to refer briefly to some of the more important aspects of current legislation at the time of writing —

31

# Town and Country Planning (Amendment) Act 1972

## CHAPTER 42

### ARRANGEMENT OF SECTIONS

*Amendments of enactments relating to development plans in England and Wales*

# Town and Country Planning Act 1971

### CHAPTER 78

LONDON
HER MAJESTY'S STATIONERY OFFICE
£1·15 net

legislation which is likely to remain effective for some years in principle although undoubtedly various modifications in interpretation and application are continually being made. The Acts themselves are in the nature of a framework within which many details are capable of change by statutory instrument.

In the following pages, unless otherwise stated, the law is that set out by the Town and Country Planning Act 1971 and the Town and Country Planning (Amendment) Act 1972, and 'planning authorities' means local planning authorities, as is the common description. The various matters referred to are only broadly explained. There are many special cases and for these and for detailed provisions, the Acts or one or more of the excellent books on planning law can be consulted.

## Planning authorities

National planning

In planning, the central government — Parliament — is primarily concerned with formulating policies and enacting legislation in the strategic, economic and social interests of the nation. This involves the taking of decisions on the distribution of available resources between the public and private sectors, between consumption and investment, and on the establishment of objectives and priorities on a national scale.

The Minister responsible for town and country planning matters in central government is known at present as the Secretary of State for the Environment. His powers and duties are considerable, although most of the executive functions are conferred, as has always been the case in this country, on local government. He has an oversight role. He is empowered to issue statutory instruments, to interpret the law, in some cases to approve decisions of local authorities, to give directions in general or particular matters, to hear appeals, and to deal with claims for compensation. He also shapes the policies of local authorities by advice and information, usually issued as circulars. Detail and day to day responsibility for planning matters rests with the Department of the Environment. This department came into existence in November 1970 and was formed by putting together three former ministries — Housing and Local Government, Public Buildings and Works, and Transport — thus concentrating under one Minister nearly all the powers to regulate

PLANNING LEGISLATION    Most land and developments in Britain are subject to planning law, which at the present time is based upon the Town and Country Planning Act 1971 and the Town and Country Planning (Amendment) Act 1972, pictured on facing page. *(photo by author with permission of the Controller of Her Majesty's Stationery Office)*

County and Metropolitan County Administration Areas of England and Wales.

Administrative Areas of Scotland.

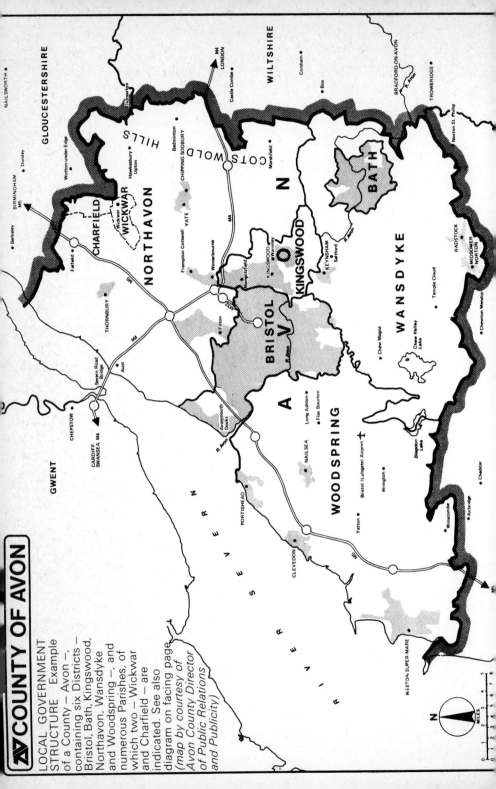

# COUNTY OF AVON

LOCAL GOVERNMENT STRUCTURE Example of a County – Avon –, containing six Districts – Bristol, Bath, Kingswood, Northavon, Wansdyke and Woodspring –, and numerous Parishes, of which two – Wickwar and Charfield – are indicated. See also diagram on facing page. (map by courtesy of Avon County Director of Public Relations and Publicity)

LOCAL GOVERNMENT STRUCTURE

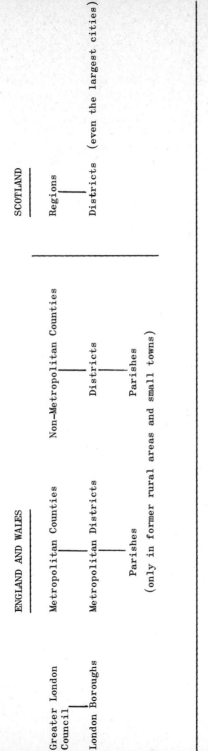

|  | ENGLAND AND WALES |  | | SCOTLAND |
|---|---|---|---|---|

Greater London Council
London Boroughs

Metropolitan Counties
Metropolitan Districts
Parishes
(only in former rural areas and small towns)

Non-Metropolitan Counties
Districts
Parishes

Regions
Districts (even the largest cities)

Examples

Counties:    AVON                                    GLOUCESTERSHIRE

Districts:    Bristol   Northavon         Cheltenham   Stroud   Gloucester

Parishes:    Wickwar   Charfield              Wotton   Kingswood

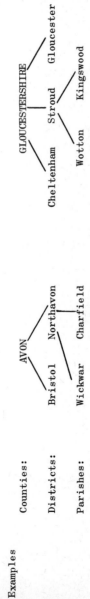

DIAGRAM OF LOCAL GOVERNMENT STRUCTURE   as reorganised for England and Wales and for Scotland –
see also maps on pp. 34–35 *(Diagram by Clr. J Heppell)*

and administer the physical environment, and thereby recognising the inter-acting nature of the wide variety of functions concerned. These functions, previously carried out by separate departments include urban and transport planning, housing and new towns, historic buildings and monuments, and building regulations. They involve raising standards and increasing the availability of housing, furthering the preservation of amenities of the countryside and historic towns, and combating pollution of land, air and water.

## Regional

A *region* is an extensive area of the country defined by a set of closely related conditions. At present, the basis of regional planning is considered to be primarily industrial development, which remains the responsibility of the Department of Trade and Industry. Certainly, employment and economics are central to regional planning, but consideration is being given to the constitution and function of regional councils which could provide a broader foundation for effective action. These councils could be representative of local government, and their function would be to discuss and determine ways of implementing central government policies and administration, as they affect their respective regions, and to co-ordinate the activities of local authorities. Meantime, some regional conferences and consultative committees have been set up jointly by local authorities to provide a regional framework for structure planning, e.g. West Midlands Regional Study and South-East Regional Study.

## Local

Under the Local Government Act 1972 which became effective in April 1974, a two-tier system of local government has been adopted in England and Wales, with a similar system in Scotland. England, outside Greater London, is divided into 6 metropolitan counties and 39 non-metropolitan counties. These metropolitan and non-metropolitan counties are further divided into 369 districts. Wales is divided into 9 counties and 36 districts, Scotland into 9 'regions' (equivalent to counties) and 53 districts.

The councils of counties and the councils of districts are the local planning authorities for their respective areas. In greater London, the Greater London Council is the local planning authority for the whole area, but within certain limits the individual councils of the London Boroughs are the local planning authorities for their respective boroughs.

Although in principle all functions conferred on local planning authorities can be exercised by county and district authorities, the principle is subject to numerous Local Government Act qualifications.

In general, therefore, the county councils are responsible for the preparation of broad planning policies, i.e. structure plans, and for related development control, and they have powers to acquire and dispose of land for development or redevelopment. In regard to housing, they are concerned with 'overspill' development. They are the authorities for highways and traffic. District councils are responsible for the preparation of local plans and for most development control. They, too, have powers to acquire and dispose of land. They are concerned with housing in many ways including the construction of dwellings, slum clearance schemes, improvement areas, and housing management. They are responsible for the maintenance of unclassified roads.

## Development plans

Among the duties of local planning authorities is the preparation of development plans. They were instructed in this respect by the Town and Country Planning Act of 1947 which set out the detailed procedure for the preparation of such plans, by which the country is still governed. Plans so prepared are known as 'old style' development plans. But a new procedure, introduced by the 1968 Act, will gradually replace them by what, obviously enough, are known as 'new style' development plans. At the time of writing they are only prepared for certain selected areas.

'Old style' development plans

These plans were required to show: (a) the manner in which the land covered by the plan is to be used, and (b) the stages by which the development is to be carried out. They comprised a basic map and a written statement; other maps, necessary for particular purposes, could be included. Plans had to be submitted to the Secretary of State for approval. Objections could be made by interested persons prior to approval, and anyone aggrieved by the approved plan could apply in certain circumstances to the High Court, which has the power to quash the plan on certain grounds. A development plan must be reviewed every five years at least, and amendments can be made by the same procedure as that for the preparation of the original plan.

'New style' development plans

The 'new style' plans entrust local planning authorities with much wider powers, the objects being to simplify procedure and to provide for greater opportunities for public participation – although this is now somewhat less that at one time envisaged. The plans are prepared in two stages: (a) Structure Plans, and (b) Local Plans.

# The Development Plan

**THE STRUCTURE PLAN**

**+**

**LOCAL PLANS**

**District Plans**
**Action Area Plans**
**Subject Plans**

A Development Plan is made up of a Structure Plan and a number of Local Plans.

These consist of written statements and diagrams or maps, with possible other information about the intentions in view.

The Structure Plan sets out the main policies to deal with the big problems, and the Local Plans give detailed proposals for parts of the Structure Plan area. Local Plans have to be in keeping with the Structure Plan.

Both Structure and Local Plans may be altered in time as people's needs change.

6

THE DEVELOPMENT PLAN    Reproduction of a poster issued by the Department of the Environment showing the relationship between Structure Plans and Local Plans – see p. 43. (Reproduced with the permission of The Controller of Her Majesty's Stationery Office.)

# The Structure Plan

A Structure Plan looks at an area in relation to the areas which surround it, and the labour, money and land likely to be available. It may be prepared for the whole or part of a county, or for a large town. Two or more planning authorities may join together and prepare one plan. The Structure Plan requires the approval of the Secretary of State.* The Structure Plan consists of a **written statement** and a **key diagram,** sometimes with other illustrations.

The **written statement** deals broadly with the way land is to be used and with matters affecting the environment. It brings together the intentions for the future on those of the following subjects which are most important to the area.

| | | |
|---|---|---|
| Population | Transport | Recreation and Leisure |
| Employment | Shopping | Conservation |
| Housing | Education | Utility Services |
| Industry | Social Services | |

Areas where big changes are proposed may be shown as **action areas.**

The **key diagram** is a guide to finding the policies for particular parts of the area in the written statement, making the plan easier to understand. The written statement will say more than the key diagram can show.

*In England, the Secretary of State for the Environment, in Wales, the Secretary of State for Wales.

**7**

STRUCTURE PLANS   Reproduction of a poster issued by the Department of the Environment describing the nature of Structure Plans which comprise a written statements and key diagrams — see p. 43. (Reproduced with the permission of the Controller of Her Majesty's Stationery Office.)

# Local Plans

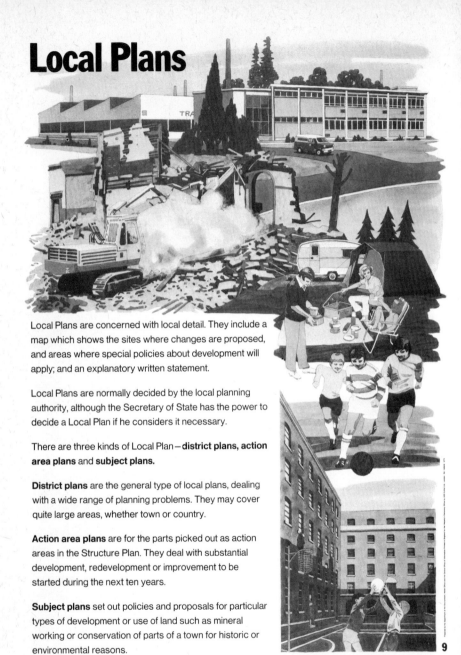

Local Plans are concerned with local detail. They include a map which shows the sites where changes are proposed, and areas where special policies about development will apply; and an explanatory written statement.

Local Plans are normally decided by the local planning authority, although the Secretary of State has the power to decide a Local Plan if he considers it necessary.

There are three kinds of Local Plan—**district plans, action area plans** and **subject plans.**

**District plans** are the general type of local plans, dealing with a wide range of planning problems. They may cover quite large areas, whether town or country.

**Action area plans** are for the parts picked out as action areas in the Structure Plan. They deal with substantial development, redevelopment or improvement to be started during the next ten years.

**Subject plans** set out policies and proposals for particular types of development or use of land such as mineral working or conservation of parts of a town for historic or environmental reasons.

9

LOCAL PLANS   Reproduction of a poster issued by the Department of the Environment describing the various types of Local Plans — see pp. 43–44. (Reproduced with the permission of The Controller of Her Majesty's Stationery Office.)

The Secretary of State has to approve structure plans, but local plans can be adopted by the local planning authorities.

## Structure plans

The structure plan is a written statement without a map, but with diagrams and other descriptive matter. It is a general statement of policy and proposals and, as it does not show how any particular parcel of land might be affected, the hope is that only problems of general policy will be discussed during the procedure leading to approval. A structure plan must show 'action areas', which are areas selected for early development, i.e. within ten years.

The general public can make representations during the preparation of structure plans as well as make objections against the draft of the completed plans, and the Secretary of State must consider all such objections prior to giving his approval. He selects those issues which he considers important and refers them to a panel of experts for examination in public in accordance with a code of practice published in 1973.

Before preparing a structure plan the local authority has to institute surveys of various kinds. Matters to be covered include data concerning the principal physical and economic characteristics of the area, population and population movement, existing land uses, communications, transport and traffic. The surveys must be kept under constant review. Two or more local authorities may combine to carry out surch surveys.

Structure plans and master plans for New Towns need to be complementary and this requires a high degree of collaboration between the authorities involved.

## Local plans

The preparation of local plans is generally regarded as the responsibility of district councils except in respect of National Park Areas, and areas for which provision has been made in the structure plan for preparation by the county authority, although in fact local plans may be prepared by either body. Local plans must be prepared as soon as possible after the structure plan has been approved. They may be prepared while the structure plan is in preparation and, in many cases, this would seem to be not only desirable but inevitable because of delays in completing the structure plan. Consequently, close co-operation between county and district authorities is essential. Cooperation is provided for by the Local Government Act 1972, which requires that county planning authorities must make and keep under review a 'Development Plan Scheme' for the preparation of local plans within their respective county areas, designating the authorities responsible for the preparation of the plans and setting out a programme for the

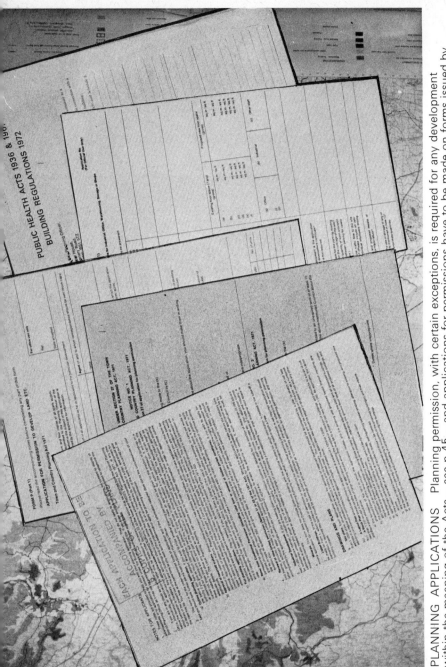

PLANNING APPLICATIONS    Planning permission, with certain exceptions, is required for any development within the meaning of the Acts – see p.45 – and applications for permissions have to be made on forms issued by the local planning authorities. The forms have to be accompanied by explanatory plans and drawings. In cases where buildings are concerned, applications for approval under Building Regulations have to be made at the same time. Examples of application forms are illustrated above. *(photo: author)*

preparation and the relationship between the plans. A copy of the scheme has to be sent to the Secretary of State who has wide powers of control in regard to the making and amendment of these schemes.

A local plan consists of a map and written statement plus other illustrations and descriptions as appropriate. The main purpose of a local plan is to guide authorities and private developers in the possible development of the land concerned. There are various kinds of local plans, varying in extent and detail. For example, district plans cover large parts of the areas of a structure plan, much smaller local plans deal with particular planning problems within a district. As with structure plans, the preparation of local plans has to be given publicity in order that interested persons can make representations for consideration, and when the plan is in draft form, time has to be allowed for any objections to be raised and, if necessary, for hearings and inquiries to be held and the points resolved before the plans are approved.

## Planning control of development

The law defines development and sets out the general principle that planning permission is required for development.

The definition of development is comprehensive and includes the carrying out of any building, engineering, mining or other operation on, over or under land, or any material change in the use of any building or land. The actual interpretation of the definition is, not surprisingly, very complex, and is subject to many qualifications. As always, one definition leads to another, and change in use in particular involves reference to further definitions of use classes* and the meaning of material change.

However, the important point is that planning permission is required for any development unless permission is expressly granted by the Act itself or by a general Development Order. The latter sets out the method of application for permissions and the procedure for dealing with applications.

Applications have to be made on a form issued by the local planning authority. The form has to be filled in to give required particulars of the proposed development and has to be accompanied by explanatory plans and drawings. The planning authority must normally give a decision within two months, or three months if a trunk road would be affected. In arriving at a decision, the authority must have regard to the relevant development plan, although in certain circumstances permission for development may be granted that it is not in accordance

* Town and Country Planning (Use Classes) Order 1972

with the development plan. The authority is empowered to impose conditions on planning permission or to grant permission for a limited period. An applicant need not necessarily have a legal interest in the land in question, that is, he need not be the owner, he can be a prospective purchaser or lessee. And if the application refers to a building project and not merely to a change of use, before going to the expense of having detailed drawings prepared, he may apply for 'outline planning permission', which can be granted subject to 'reserved matters', i.e. the actual siting and design of the building. Once outline planning permission has been granted, further planning permission cannot later be refused on grounds outside the reserved matters.

### Appeals against planning decisions

Anyone aggrieved by the refusal of a planning authority to approve a development or by the imposition of conditions has the right of appeal to the Secretary of State. The appeal has to be made within the time allowed by the General Development Order, that is, six months. Appeals may be allowed or dismissed, or part of the planning authority's decision may be reversed or varied even if it is not a subject of the appeal. Consequently, it can happen that by making an appeal the applicant is putting the whole issue for consideration and the Secretary of State's decision may be less favourable in other matters than that which gave rise to the appeal! Before deciding an appeal, opportunity must be given, on the request of either party, that is, the applicant and the planning authority, for both to be heard by an Inspector. Inquiries may be private but are usually public, especially for more important appeals. Some appeals, as set out in the Town and Country Planning (Determination of Appeals by Appointed Persons) (Prescribed Classes) Regulations, are in any case determined not by the Secretary of State but by an Inspector appointed by him. The procedure is much the same as for appeals heard by the Secretary of State and the Inspector's decision has the same validity.

### Duration of planning permission

There are two limitations in the time attached to planning permissions. (a) the development must start within the statutory period – usually five years unless the planning authority has specified a shorter period, and (b) if completion is unduly delayed the planning authority can issue a 'completion notice' revoking the permission on expiration of a further reasonable period of time being not less than twelve months. Such notice has to be confirmed by the Secretary of State.

In respect of outline planning permission, application for approval of 'reserved matters' must be made within three years and the development must commence within five years from the granting of outline planning permission, or two years from approval of reserved matters, whichever is the later.

Discontinuance of use or alternation or removal of buildings or works

The planning authority can issue an order (with approval of the Secretary of State) requiring the discontinuance of use or the alteration or removal of buildings or works, but in such cases compensation has to be paid.

Conservation areas

Local planning authorities have a duty to determine which parts of their respective areas are of special architectural or historic interest, and to designate such as 'conservation areas'. The Secretary of State can also direct the designation of conservation areas. There are nearly 3000 conservation areas in Britain.

Legal provisions relating to conservation areas include mandatory prominent publicity of applications for development that might adversely affect the character or appearance of a conservation area, so that the public are aware of the issues and can raise objections. The powers of the Secretary of State to direct planning authorities to consult with other persons or bodies in considering applications, and the powers of control exercisable by the authority over the demolition of any building in a conservation area, even though it is not a listed building, are referred to below.

## Special planning control

Buildings of architectural or historic interest

Lists of buildings of interest are compiled by the Secretary of State. These lists are supplied to planning authorities, and the owners of the buildings are notified. Ancient monuments and churches are otherwise protected.

The legal consequence of listing is that any act causing damage to a listed building is an offence punishable by a fine. It is an offence to demolish, alter or extend such a building without obtaining a 'listed building consent', which is distinct from normal planning permission. A listed building which is not being properly preserved can be compulsorily acquired by the planning authority or the Secretary of State after a due 'repair notice' has proved ineffective. Compensation is payable, but if the building has been deliberately neglected only 'minimum compensation', which excludes any profit that might derive from development of the site, is payable.

There are set procedures in the application for listed building consent, in dealing with applications, in appeals against decisions, and in other matters related thereto.

## Trees
Planning authorities in granting planning permission must endeavour, where such action is appropriate, to preserve existing trees or to require the planting of new trees. They also have a duty to issue 'tree preservation orders' if, in the interests of amenity, it is desirable to preserve particular trees or groups of trees or woodland. Contravention of a tree preservation order is an offence punishable by a fine.

## Advertisements
Advertisements are widely defined by planning legislation and, although there are certain commonsense exceptions, their display is severely restricted and controlled. In areas of 'special control' — rural areas or areas or particular amenity — advertisements may be completely disallowed or allowed only within strict limits. The controlling authority is the district planning authority. Any person displaying an advertisement in contravention of the regulations can be fined. Provision is made for applying for express consent, and for appeals against adverse decisions.

## Waste land
If a planning authority considers that the amenities of their area are seriously affected by the unsatisfactory condition of any open space, including private gardens, a notice requiring abatement of the condition can be served on the owner or occupier of the land. Failing compliance, an enforcement notice can be served by the planning authority, as in other cases of contravention of planning control (see p. 52).

## Industrial development
Apart from certain exceptions, a local planning authority cannot consider an application in connection with the development of land for the erection of an industrial building unless it is accompanied by an 'Industrial Development Certificate' (IDC) issued by the Secretary of State, confirming that the proposed development is consistent with the proper distribution of industry having particular regard to the need for providing employment in development areas. An IDC may impose conditions to this end.

THE CARAVAN PROBLEM   An almost incredible picture of a huge caravan 'park' occupying a large coastal area. *(photo: West Air Photography)*

Office development

In an area where the provisions apply (at present they apply to South-East England) applications for planning permission in respect of office development exceeding 10 000 ft² whether by way of new building or by change of use must be accompanied by an 'Office Development Permit' (ODP) issued by the Secretary of State, whose powers are similar to those he has in industrial development.

Caravans

Caravan sites pose a potential threat to the amenity of their neighbouring areas and are therefore subject to dual control. Firstly, a developer must obtain planning permission for the use of the proposed site — this is usually a matter of change of use, and second, he must obtain a 'site licence' as required by the Caravan Sites and Control of Development Act 1960. Site licences are issued by the local housing authority, i.e. the district council, and must be granted if planning permission has been granted. However, the significance of the licence lies in the conditions that it can impose. These conditions are what the authority considers necessary or desirable in the interests of the caravan dwellers, and any other persons affected, such as neighbours and the general public. In addition, regulations must cover the number, siting and types of caravans permitted, provision of sanitary facilities, fire precautions, amenities, etc. A developer aggrieved by conditions may appeal to a magistrates' court.

## Acquisition of land

Acquisition by compulsory purchase

Local authorities have far-reaching legal powers for the compulsory acquisition of land for development, redevelopment or improvement in the general public interest, or because the land is required for relocation of population or industry or the replacement of open space. The Secretary of State may also compulsorily acquire land for public purposes or acquire an easement or other rights over land. There are special provisions in regard to the compulsory acquisition of listed buildings.

Acquisition by agreement

Local authorities may also acquire land or buildings in certain circumstances by agreement or exchange, and in such cases conveyance is effected as it is between private parties.

Development of acquired land

Where local authority has acquired land, it can either develop the land or dispose of it to a developer, who himself has no powers of compulsory purchase but who is prepared to develop the land in an approved manner. The Secretary of State may specify a developer, but only for the best price reasonably obtainable. Disposal has to ensure, so far as practicable, that persons formerly living or carrying on business on the land concerned will be able to get suitable accommodation at a suitable price in the new development. Much land has been developed in this way in recent years.

## Agreements regulating development or use of land

A planning authority is empowered to enter into an agreement with persons interested in land in its area, and restrict or regulate development either permanently or for a certain period on such terms and conditions as appear to the authority to be expedient. In some cases, it appears that the granting of planning permission for a commercial development has been part of a bargain or 'package deal', whereby a developer in return for permission not only accepts certain conditions but actually donates part of his land or otherwise assists the authority in road improvement or housing. Proposals for such dealing are likely to be instigated by development companies primarily in their own interest, but they may well be acceptable to local authorities in present circumstances. However, there have been some cases that have given rise to public concern where the private development has been attacked on social and environmental grounds.

## Enforcement of control

Laws are of little use unless they can be enforced. Planning legislation provides for enforcement by enabling planning authorities to serve an 'enforcement notice' where there appears to have been a breach of planning control. A breach of planning control is not a criminal offence but non-compliance with an enforcement order is, and is punishable.

An enforcement notice can be served on any person having an interest in the land concerned. Severe fines can be imposed on convicted persons and in addition they may become liable for continuing daily fines if they fail to discontinue a prohibited use of land or fail to do everything within their power as soon as possible to comply with the enforcement order.

Appeals against an enforcement order can be made in certain circumstances to the Secretary of State. But to prevent the continuance of the alleged breach of planning control while appeals and other proceedings are being disposed of (which could be a lengthy business) the planning authority can issue a 'stop notice' with or after the enforcement order to stop immediately some kinds of development, but not a change of use unless the deposit of waste material is involved. Contravention of provisions in the control over listed buildings or of a tree preservation order or over waste land can lead, on conviction, not only to fines but in the event of continued non-compliance to the planning authority taking remedial action and to recovering the cost thereof from the offender. This applies also to unauthorised display of advertisements, and to failure to discontinue unauthorised use of land and the alteration or removal of unauthorised buildings.

## Planning inquiries

In many instances when the decisions or action of planning authorities are challenged, public inquiries may be held. The procedure and conduct of public inquiries on planning matters are governed by two sets of similar rules: one is applicable where the appeal is to be determined by the Secretary of State, and the other where it is to be determined by an Inspector.

## Compensation

There are many instances, some of which have been mentioned, where action by planning authorities entitles the person affected to compensation because he cannot use his land in the most profitable manner or suffers loss in some other way. Some of the categories of planning action which can, in certain circumstances, give rise to compensation are planning decisions prohibiting or restricting new development, orders requiring the discontinuance of use or requiring the alteration or removal of buildings or works, orders relating to listed buildings or tree preservation, and restrictions on advertisements.

There is also the general principal in Britain, that when land is compulsorily acquired compensation has to be paid.

### Compulsory acquisition

The Land Compensation Act 1961 lays down rules for assessing compensation when land is compulsorily acquired. These take into account not only the value of the land, but also compensation for 'disturbance', i.e. cost of removal and similar incidental expenses which the owner may incur consequent upon loss of use of the land, and compensation for 'injurious affection', i.e. for owners who have land held with but not necessarily adjoining the land taken that is depreciated in value. Compensation may also be payable in a lesser degree to other persons who are affected by the compulsory acquisition.

Lands tribunal

Any question of disputed compensation arising from compulsory acquisition of land must be referred to and determined by the Lands Tribunal, a body set up under the Lands Tribunal Act 1949. This body can also act on questions of compensation in other cases where valuation of land is involved.

## Purchase notice by owners

Because of planning restrictions, land may become of no value to the owner or his interest in it may be seriously affected. In such circumstances he has the right to ask the planning authority to purchase the land. He does this by serving a 'purchase notice' on grounds of either (a) adverse planning decision, or (b) adverse planning proposal.

Adverse planning decisions

If the owner claims that his land has been rendered incapable of beneficial use in its existing state or because of conditions attached to planning permission, and cannot be rendered capable by any permitted development, he can serve a notice to purchase, with which the planning authority can comply either by buying the land themselves or by finding another authority or statutory undertaker to do so. Failing compliance, the matter must be referred to the Secretary of State who has to approve the notice before it can become operative. He may, however, grant permission for the unrestricted development sought by the owner or for some other development that would render the land capable of beneficial use.

A purchase notice can also be served by an owner on revocation or modification of planning permission, or if the authority issues an order requiring discontinuance of use or the alteration or removal of buildings or works. Similarly, a notice can be served on refusal or consent of a listed building or of a tree preservation order, or if permission to display an advertisement is denied.

Adverse planning proposals (planning blight)

Where the interests of an owner-occupier are affected by planning proposals to the extent that the land is rendered unsaleable or saleable only at a very low price, then it is considered fair that he should be enabled to issue a purchase notice. The Act gives a number of circumstances, all of which may be described as cases where the land may be required at some future date for a public purpose, e.g. a new highway. There are various conditions that have to be fulfilled by the owner-occupier, or the planning authority can object to the notice.

If the authority does not comply within two months from the serving of the notice, the owner-occupier can require the matter to be referred to the Lands Tribunal. If the notice is confirmed, compensation is the price of the unblighted land plus any additional amount for disturbance or injurious affection.

It is the district planning authority that pays compensation when a purchase notice is served and confirmed.

# 4
# Planning in Practice

## The agencies of planning

This chapter discusses the organisation and persons directly concerned with environmental planning at different levels and in various situations, and describes how planning legislation is implemented.

Some environmental problems, such as marine pollution and the exploitation or conservation of certain natural resources, call for action on an international scale. At present a supra-national planning agency is unlikely, although specialised sections of international organisations, e.g. United Nations and European Economic Community, are likely to play an increasing role in promoting conferences and discussions for the exchange of ideas and information which may lead to agreements on restrictive, remedial or other action.

Most planning, however, is a matter of national, regional and local concern. The two main agencies or instruments of planning in Britain are those of central and local government.

Central government
The work of the central government, operating through the Department of the Environment, was outlined in the previous chapter.

Regional bodies
The work of regional administrative and consultative bodies was also referred to in Chapter 3. They are sometimes regarded as a kind of 'provincial government', needed for dealing with those matters that cannot be effectively handled by local authorities and yet, by reason of differing conditions of the regions concerned, require a more limited

degree of planning action than that at the national level. Nevertheless, while there may well be in the future some strengthening of these bodies for particular purposes it would seem that their function will always be in the nature of intermediaries between central and local government and not as separate planning authorities on a full and permanent basis.

## Local government

County and District Councils are the authorities chiefly concerned with planning at the level at which it effects real development and thereby the every day environment in which we live. The responsibilities and duties of the two tiers of local government have been discussed. There is no uniformity of organisation. The various local authorities have different problems to face and their approaches are by no means the same. The political constitution of each council has considerable effect on its policies and decisions.

In general, the council appoints or elects a planning committee consisting of members of the council having special knowledge of or interest in planning, but the day to day work is carried out by a planning department (see later).

It should first be mentioned that planning in the sense of implementation of planning legislation is only one of the activities of a local authority. Because all its activities are inter-related there has emerged what is known as 'corporate planning', which can be defined as the integration of all local government action in dealing with the social, economic and physical problems of an area. Corporate planning is important not only at country or strategic level to ensure compatible action between policies and practices at that level, but also at district level, since the success of new development or redevelopment depends upon co-ordinated community planning, involving social services, housing management, environmental maintenance, etc., as well as upon physical design.

In this connection, major authorities need a policy planning unit to advise the council on central government policies and the overall local situation. Such a unit relies upon constituent departments of the authority for information, which it carefully analyses and interprets. The planning department also has a significant role. Routine 'feedback' from development control, which deals with applications for planning permission, provides valuable information indicative of changes in demand for various kinds of development.

## Planning departments

A planning department usually consists of permanent officials, i.e.

non-political appointments, commonly a principal planning officer, a deputy planning officer, a number of assistant planning officers, and a staff of assistant planners and technicians of various grades, amongst whom are those with specialist qualifications and experience. Outside consultants are sometimes engaged to assist with the department's work in particular areas, e.g. conservation.

The work of a planning department falls into two main categories — the preparation of development plans for the future, and development control. The former is now thoroughly prescribed by current legislation, the dual system of structure and local plans, the object of which is to allocate land and direct development in accordance with an integrated pattern of economic, social and environmental needs.

Development plans

The preparation of development plans is comprehensively described in a central government publication entitled *Development Plans — A Manual of Form and Content.* This book provides clearly and with ample illustrations the various kinds of plans and their presentation of policies and proposals. It is primarily a reference document to guide planning authorities, and is divided into three parts:

1. a description of the development plan system as a whole,
2. a detailed explanation of structure plans, and
3. a detailed explanation of local plans.

It is of interest to mention some of the things dealt with as they are of importance in contributing to an understanding of how official planning is actually carried out.

The section on the plan system discusses the relationship between structure and local plans, including the types and functions of each of the latter. It emphasises that all development plans must be flexible enough to cover all the matters that are subject to planning control and influence in varying degrees of detail and at differing time-scales (periods over which development may take place), and must consider financial implications. It defines common terms, as, for example, 'diagram' — a generalised cartographic expression of an idea drawn only approximately to scale, or 'map' — precise planning information drawn accurately to scale usually over an Ordnance Sheet base. The word 'plan' means a description by any means of aims, policies and proposals.

It points out that the preparation of plans involves consultation and co-ordination with and between various local authorities and govern-ment departments, regional planning bodies, statutory undertakers (gas and electricity boards, etc.), nationalised industries, and, as expressly required by legislation, with the general public and representa-

# DEVELOPMENT PLANS

CHARACTERISTIC NOTATIONS

Ministry of Housing and Local Government

Welsh Office

London    Her Majesty's Stationery Office    1970

Price 5s 0d [25p] net

# DEVELOPMENT PLANS

A MANUAL ON FORM AND CONTENT

tive public organisations. This parallels to some extent what is known as 'community planning', which is a separate activity rather wider in scope than structure planning or corporate planning in that it is concerned in depth with all agencies whose activities in any way affect the lives of members of a particular or supposed community.

Since changes may require plans to be amended, repealed or replaced, the system identifies the areas that have to be studied and re-examined in order to ensure the validity of data, of information and of the assumptions upon which the plans are based.

It encourages the issue of informal documents for the guidance of intending developers to provide them with criteria for acceptable layouts and building design.

Structure plans

The Manual describes the statutory provisions of these plans which are intended in the first instance to establish a ten-year or longer programme involving considerations of such activities as employment, shopping, education and recreation, and their respective spheres of influence (which do not necessarily coincide with one another nor with local authority boundaries). The purposes of structure plans are listed, and the headings give a very good idea of what they are all about:

1. interpreting national and regional policies
2. establishing aims, policies and general proposals
3. providing a framework for local plans
4. indicating action areas
5. providing guidance for development control
6. providing a basis for coordinating decisions
7. bringing main planning issues before the Minister and the public.

It points out that structure plans are to be described in words, and the form and content of written statements is dealt with at length. Standardisation is considered to be inappropriate, but all structure plans will have certain common features; the normal range is given and guidance is provided in the scope of policies for areas, sub-areas and action areas. It recommends that general illustration of the strategy should be by

DEVELOPMENT PLANS MANUAL   The preparation of development by local authorities, see p. 39, is comprehensively described in a Government publication illustrated above. The manual includes examples of the various kinds of development maps, diagrams and other drawings, with recommended notations (representations), colours, etc. *(photo by author with permission of the Controller of Her Majesty's Stationery Office)*

means of a 'key diagram', of which examples are shown, with such other illustrations as necessary for clarification, and again examples are given.

Local plans

The Manual describes the statutory provisions and elucidates the three kinds of local plans: district, action area and subject.

A district plan is for the comprehensive planning of relatively large areas which are likely to be developed piecemeal over a long period.

An action area plan is for the comprehensive planning for those areas indicated in the structure plan where development or redevelopment is expected to take place within ten years.

Subject plans are for dealing with particular aspects in advance of comprehensive planning or where a comprehensive plan is not needed. All local plans have as their function:

1. application of the strategy of structure plans,
2. provision of a detailed basis for development control,
3. provision of a basis for co-ordinating developments, and
4. the bringing of local and detailed planning issues before the public.

The Manual discusses various matters relevant to the preparation of local plans, e.g. the making of decisions, the exercise of control, public acquisition of land, housing improvement, and conservation areas. As with structure plans, the form and content of local plans is covered in detail. The preparation of various kinds of maps, diagrams and other drawings, with recommended notations, symbols, colours, etc., is also discussed. Although these ways of presentation are not obligatory it is obviously advantageous that uniformity greatly facilitates the 'reading' and understanding of such documents.

Development control

The other main branch of work carried out by planning departments is the exercise of planning control, whereby the activities of developers, public and private, is regulated.

The practice has remained virtually unchanged for some years and is generally regarded as having worked well. However, at the time of writing, the system is under review. From an interim report* it would seem that no fundamental alteration is envisaged, but further consideration following reactions to the provisional conclusions and recommendations may result in rather more far-reaching changes. Criticisms of the existing system, thought by some to be too rigid and

* *Review of Development Control System; Interim Report,* G. Dobry, QC.

bureaucratic, have been directed mainly towards:

1. Delays in dealing with applications and with appeals
   (in some measure this has been due to the greatly increased number of applications during times of building boom, and to the greatly increased number of appeals as both developers and the public became aware of their rights in this respect. The situation is exacerbated by shortage of qualified staff resulting partly from local government reorganisation, and partly because of the utilisation of available staff for the preparation of 'new style' development plans, as well as to the growing demand for higher standards of environmental design which makes control more difficult).

2. Using of 'old style' development plans as the basis of control (as 'new style' development plans are introduced and preliminary studies become available, this complaint will presumably diminish).

3. Disagreement with decisions on aesthetic grounds; good but progressive architectural designs sometimes refused, while bad or indifferent conventional designs permitted.

4. Inadequacy of public participation in the development control process
   (this appears due to lack of publicity in regard to potentially controversial developments, and failure to take into account local conservation societies' attitudes).

To meet these criticisms, it is not proposed that there should be any substantial relaxation of control, but it is accepted that there should be a speeding up and simplification of the process. Aesthetic control could be abated and designs by qualified architects not challenged provided, it is to be hoped, that the commonly accepted criteria of good urban design are observed. Clear policy guidance and publication of performance requirements, and perhaps the issue of informal plans for the benefit of those small developers without benefit of proper professional advice could do a great deal to save time by reducing the number of totally unsuitable initial applications. Minor residential applications, which comprise a large proportion of applications, might be dealt with more quickly by a simplification of documentation and procedure in such cases. In almost all instances, prior discussion and perhaps negotiation between prospective developers and planning control staff could be helpful. As regards developments of a nature likely to give rise to public concern, better means of informing interested persons and local organisations should be adopted. This need not be done in such a way as to invite adverse criticism or opposition but to make perfectly clear what is proposed.

## Other bodies concerned with planning

The Government

The Department of the Environment is the principal Government body dealing with planning, but there are many other official departments and organisations with responsibilities wholly or partly concerned with various aspects. Prominent amongst these are:

Central Housing Advisory Committee

Centre for Environmental Studies — an independent body for promoting and publishing research into problems of urban and regional planning; it provides a forum for discussions of matters of common interest to planners and research workers.

Commission for the New Towns

Countryside Commission — set up under the Countryside Act 1968 absorbing the earlier National Parks Commission, it has a wide range of advisory and executive functions relating to the whole of the countryside and the coast in England and Wales (there is a similar Countryside Commission for Scotland); all matters concerned with the provision of facilities for the enjoyment of the countryside, conservation and public access for recreation are its province; it is the designator of National Parks, of which there are now 10, and smaller Areas of Outstanding Natural Beauty, of which there are 28. Administration of National Parks by County planning authorities is subject to supervision by the Countryside Commission.

Department of Health and Social Security

Forestry Commission — an agency which promotes the interests of forestry on a national scale; nearly two million acres of land have been planted.

Nature Conservancy — establishes and manages nature reserves in Great Britain. Sites of special scientific interest are notified to local planning authorities, who have a duty to consult the Nature Conservancy when planning applications affect such sites.

New Towns Development Corporations — public bodies whose members are appointed by the Secretary of State for the Environment to undertake the development of New Towns; they prepare master plans, employ planning and other staff and carry out actual developments; when population growth is substantially complete, the Commission for the New Towns takes over.

Ordnance Survey — the official mapping organisation of Great Britain responsible for the publication of maps to various scales providing considerable physical information about the country. The maps are extensively used in planning.

Royal Fine Arts Commission — a permanent body to which important matters of public amenity or aesthetic importance may be referred for advice and recommendation; it is sometimes called to look into designs for new public buildings. The Royal Fine Arts Commission for Scotland has similar terms of reference in regard to that country.

Scottish National Housing and Town Planning Council — formed to enlist the interest and support of local authorities and others in securing housing of good standards in Scotland, and to encourage the preparation of town planning schemes.

Welsh Office — established to deal with Welsh Affairs through the Secretary of State for Wales, including planning information services.

Preservation and conservation societies

There are many national, regional and local organisations in Britain concerned with various aspects of preservation and conservation. Prominent amongst them are:

Civic Trust — an independent amenity organisation with the objectives of encouraging high quality architecture and planning, preserving buildings of distinction or historic interest, protecting the beauties of the countryside and 'inter alia' stimulating public interest in the good appearance of town and country. There are similar bodies in Scotland and Wales.

Council for the Protection of Rural England — acts as a centre for the giving of advice and information on matters affecting the protection of rural scenery from disfigurement and injury. There is a similar Council for Wales.

National Trust — promotes the permanent preservation for the nation's benefit of buildings of historic interest and land of natural beauty.

Private planning consultants

Although most environmental planning is carried out by qualified planners and other specialists in government service, there are many private consultants working in Britain, some with operations abroad, especially in developing countries.

The work of consultants covers a wide field. It includes advising developers on planning procedure and the preparation of planning applications, and advising landowners and property owners on the effect that planning proposals may have on their interests. They may themselves prepare plans for both rural and urban areas to cover development proposals for individual sites up to large-scale schemes for town expansion or renewal. Some combine planning with the practice of architecture and design residential and industrial estates.

Central and local government planning departments may engage consultants from time to time in connection with specialist surveys which are outside the experience of their officers or the capacities of their staffs, e.g. traffic and transport problems, unusual redevelopment areas, and conservation studies. On issues that have raised public concern, the independent assessment that private consultants can provide may be of benefit.

## Information gathering and handling

For the design process in planning, i.e. the formulation of policies and proposals, reliable information is essential. Much of this information is obtained by means of surveys.

### Surveys

Surveys in the planning sense can be described as the collection, sorting and interpreting of data. The execution of such surveys is obligatory by legislation on local planning authorities, and is also required at national and regional levels, and in connection with the development of New Towns.

Some of the subjects commonly studied are: physical characteristics and resources of the area concerned, existing land uses, patterns of urban growth or decline, age and condition of buildings, communication systems and traffic, industry and employment, population constituents and movements, and social conditions and attitudes. In addition, special studies may be necessary for particular purposes, e.g. for a conservation area or for a country park.

County planning departments may employ a number of variously qualified research workers, often graduates in geography, to carry out the surveys. District departments may have only a few such specialists and may share personnel with other districts or make use of County staff. Outside consultants may be engaged for difficult surveys or surveys requiring expert knowledge.

Surveys have to be carefully organised and the collection of information and its sorting and interpretation carried out as objectively and free from prejudice as possible.

The first stage is the drawing up of a precise statement of requirements in a scientific manner. Exploratory studies or pilot surveys may be necessary to establish the best way of setting about a particular inquiry.

TECHNIQUES  Computer science plays an important role in the utilisation of mathematical modelling techniques in present-day planning practice — see p. 67.
The illustration above includes examples of two operational systems: a punched card from a survey data programme, and a portion of perforated tape from a transportation study.
*(computer room design by author; card and tape supplied by A K McCarthy)*

The actual method employed will depend upon the aim of the survey, the nature of the situation, and the available sources of information. It may be a matter of observation and physical investigation, a circulation of questionnaires, personal interviews, an examination of existing material of a similar kind, or a combination of more than one method. While thoroughness is manifestly desirable, because of limitations of manpower or financial resources — some surveys can be time-consuming and expensive — adequate information can be obtained in certain cases by various sampling techniques utilising either a carefully chosen representative section or a random selection as appropriate.

After the information has been gathered, it has to be analysed and presented in a suitable manner, by graphs, charts, maps, diagrams, tables, etc., from which conclusions can be drawn and informed assumptions made. From the analyses, data also become available for use in connection with sophisticated techniques as described later.

Surveys are essential not only in policy formulation, but also in monitoring the results of implementation; re-surveys or new surveys are a necessary part of the continuous process of critical examination of policies and the consideration of amendments in the light of experience and changing conditions.

Modelling techniques

In the last decade there has been an increasing use of mathematical or quantitative models* in planning practice, due in part to the acceptance of the 'systems view' idea. The operation of these models is a highly specialised subject, but one of considerable importance in the present-day scene.

The models are a formulation or expression in mathematical terms or symbols of real world situations, although necessarily in simplified manner. They have several uses. They are of value in indicating the probable effects and thereby the acceptability of possible solutions to specific planning problems and so provide more precise guidelines for the determination of development proposals. They can also be used to observe and monitor the effects of implementation from time to time. In short, they are tools for the planner, complementing traditional methods of analysis and forecasting but not dispensing with the need for expert judgement in the making of final decisions. At all times they have to be employed with an appreciation of their limitations as well as their potentialities and with a deep understanding of the real world situation.

Mathematical models are usually classified as:

Descriptive — dealing with features of an existing urban environment, expressing them in mathematical language and so providing a means of ascertaining difficult-to-survey data from known related information.

Predictive or Forecasting — simulates future situations, i.e. illustrates probable results of the taking of certain action.

Planning or Normative — extends predictive models to show not only what may happen as a result of certain action, but also what range of performance is possible in relation to defined objectives.

* The word 'model' is used here in the abstract sense. Physical models, i.e. scaled-down tangible replicas of layouts and buildings are referred to on p. 70. Both meanings of the word relate to representations of reality.

There are many types of models. Some of the better known are:

Linear — a fairly simple type; an example of its use would be the estimating of regional growth or distribution of population within the region from the assumption that population change is primarily related to employment opportunities.

Gravity — the type most used in planning and transport studies is based on the interaction or 'attraction' between urban areas; it can be employed for a number of purposes such as predicting journey-to-work trips, and determining the effect of a new out-of-town shopping centre.

'Lowry' — a method that is less complicated than some but, originally at least, static in that it describes the urban system at one point in time. There are later variations.

Optimising — a type used when the object is to find the best use for an area of land or some other development value from a number of alternative possibilities.

Much research and refinement continues into the application of existing models and the development of new models. For the present, it is recognised that forecasting is in many cases unnecessarily difficult and it is costly to attempt to attain a high degree of accuracy. Mostly it is sufficient for general indications to be ascertained, especially in what are termed 'qualitative' or 'directional' forecasts. There is always the possibility of unforeseen or new factors arising which can upset predictions. They should therefore be used for relatively short periods, and be kept under review for any revision that may become necessary owing to changed conditions, or as improved data becomes available.

Computers

Computer science plays a major rôle in both the expression and the operation of the above-mentioned mathematically-based simulation modelling techniques. The chief characteristic of computers is their ability to perform calculations at high speed and with mechanical accuracy. All operational urban models rely upon computers for their efficient use since they involve too much monotonous repetitive calculation to be conveniently utilised, or perhaps utilised at all, if only ordinary arithmetic or hand-calculators are available. In addition, computers enable much more complicated urban relationships to be conceived and evaluated.

Computers are also used in planning for the analysis of survey data, which can then be stored for future reference.

## Communication

From the highly specialised techniques of mathematical modelling

ORDNANCE SURVEY MAPS   Maps prepared by the Ordnance Survey are extensively used in planning practice. Such maps are produced at various scales and for various purposes. The illustration at the left is a reproduction of plan ST5874 (National Grid reference no.) at scale: 1:2500 or 25.344 inches to 1 mile showing a built up area of Bristol, included in the aerial photograph on p. 22. Redland Court, now a girls' school, was an eighteenth-century mansion and the avenue of trees that once led to the entrance remain in what is now public open space. Most of the land of the estate was sold for houses in the nineteenth-century and was laid out as indicated. The photograph above is a general view of the stereo-plotting department at the Ordnance Survey establishment, Southampton. *(photo: courtesy of Information Officer, Ordnance Survey)*

and computer science, a turn now to the older but always essential graphical skills used in planning practice. Communication internally amongst professionals, technicians and others, and between planners and politicians and the general public involves not only the spoken and written words but also, and to a very large extent, graphics. All concerned directly with planning require an understanding of such media, and some need a degree of skill in their preparation and use. Technicians and draughtsmen are mainly responsible for the making of more finished works, particularly those that are large and intricate, but the whole planning process from the compilation and analysis of survey data to the formulation of designs involves illustration of one kind or another and the conveyance of ideas by graphical means.

Drawings

Foremost amongst graphic representation are maps and diagrams which depict such things as existing topography, soil conditions, land uses, roads, and railways, and corresponding maps and diagrams showing planning proposals. Many maps of the latter kind are prepared on or from Ordnance Survey sheets, which are the principal examples of the former.

There are well-established conventions for planning maps and drawings. The previously mentioned 'Development Plans' manual sets out recommended styles and notations for the various types of drawings which have to be prepared by planning authorities. As well as typical examples, different kinds of lines, hatchings, edgings, etc., the uses of letter and combinations of letters are given.

The majority of planning drawings are two-dimensional representations, i.e. maps or what are commonly called 'plans' in the orthographic sense, but there are cases when these representations are supplemented by scale projections which give pictorial impressions. The most common of these is axonometric projection, often used in the portrayal of buildings and urban developments generally. Perspective drawings also are much used for similar purposes as, for example, the appearance of a proposed shopping precinct or for the study of new buildings in relation to existing ones. Perspective drawings range from simple black and white freehand sketches to carefully prepared drawings, sometimes made with the aid of computers, highly finished in colour so that they are almost photographic in their realistic illustration of proposed developments.

Scale models

Physical scaled-down models made of wood, card, plastic and all kinds of materials are extensively used in planning practice to show existing areas and proposed developments.

In the early stages of the design process, models are valuable in relating areas of land use, the disposition of roads and other communications, the siting of buildings, etc., in a way that makes it easier to appreciate the possibilities and potentialities of proposals. Different arrangements can be manipulated quickly and sometimes more effectively than in other media. Small blocks of material can be moved about and can be viewed and photographed from various angles for comparative study and record. When a development is to be carried out in stages, models can be used to illustrate progress to ultimate fulfilment with possible modifications 'en route'.

Also in regard to design, the act of making a model, as with a drawing, is productive of ideas and suggestive of solutions to problems. Design process models need not be elaborate nor over-realistic, but they must be in scale and basically accurate in size.

To illustrate proposed developments or completed works for public presentation or exhibition, scale models are usually made in greater detail and with more realism. Such models require professional skill and experience and although some large planning authorities and private consultants have model makers on their staffs, independent experts are often employed.

Photography

Photography is used in many ways in planning practice: in data collection, in communication, and in designing among other purposes. Surveys of land areas are made or assisted by photography. Aerial photographs are taken for speed, especially of difficult terrain and remote regions. Considerable accuracy can be achieved, and systems of photogrammetry enable contours to be automatically produced on drawings. Photographs at lower level are taken to show existing conditions as required. They may be used to record historic buildings or the character of conservation areas including interesting views from within or from outside the areas.

In a different context, cameras can take and record pictures of things which the human eye cannot conveniently see, if see at all, as, for example, wind tunnel effects to demonstrate air movement on and about buildings and other structures.

Various kinds of photographs, including large-scale enlargements and photomontage, are used for exhibition display to illustrate planning proposals for public viewing and other explanatory purposes. Transparencies in black and white or in colour can be projected in a number of ways, in some cases producing stereoscopic effects.

In the synthetic stage of physical design, photographs can be used

LAS CUEVAS ESTATE DEVELOP

CARIBBEAN RESORTS (TRINIDAD) LIM

SCALE MODELS  Physical scaled-down models are extensively used in planning practice at various stages of the design process and to illustrate proposed developments or complete works.

The photograph above shows a built-up model of a hilly coastal site for a resort indicating roads and footpaths, residential areas, sites for shopping centre, school, public buildings and hotel, etc. See also p. 78.

To the right are photographs showing the use of the Modelscope, an optical device which used by itself enables the viewer to observe scenes within a model as if on an actual site, or used in conjunction with still, motion picture or television cameras enables visual effects to be recorded for further study. *(photos: courtesy of Specfield Limited)*

to put together spatial elements derived from scale models or drawings for the study of alternative solutions. Sometimes this is done by combining photographs and drawings. For example, a drawing of a proposed urban development may be superimposed on an enlarged photograph of the actual site, brought to the same scale.

Motion pictures can be employed for the same purposes as still photography, but with a greater degree of realism. Wide, sweeping shots of landscape or other environmental conditions can be more effective at times than a series of ordinary photographs. The range and coverage of subjects is widely extended, and both slow motion and accelerated pictures may be used to illustrate particular aspects of traffic, vehicular and pedestrian movement, etc. Spoken commentaries and sound effects can be added for educational purposes and public presentation.

Motion pictures made in conjunction with the 'modelscope', a device for viewing scenes within scale models as though the viewer were actually seeing them life-size, provide a means of studying three-dimensional visual design with greater realism. Closed circuit television can also be used with the modelscope for immediate viewing, and a recording for later reproduction can be made on tape.

# 5
# Planning Issues

There are a number of fairly well-defined planning issues, as they may be termed, often of a controversial nature, that receive attention constantly, and which in relation to current events are dealt with in one way or another, not only at official conferences and meetings but also by public discussion, commonly promoted by the press, radio and television.

Amongst them are such issues as: public participation in planning, transport and traffic, politics and planning, planning for leisure, inner city redevelopment, and out-of-town shopping centres. These are so frequently debated and commented upon, that it is felt unnecessary to further refer to them directly. However, the subjects of the following pages touch upon such issues, and in so doing indicate some of the questions with which government, professionals and the general public have continually to consider. The selected subjects are: new towns, rural planning, ecology and pollution, urban preservation and conservation, and visual aspects of planning. There are many actual and implied cross-references between these individual issues, and between them and the contents of the earlier chapters of this book, thus again showing the interaction and interrelationships of the various elements that go to make up the total planning picture.

**NEW TOWNS** Map showing locations of New Towns in England, Wales, Scotland and Northern Ireland in 1974.

**New towns**

New towns have been planned at all periods of history for one reason or another — for the establishment of colonies, as administrative centres, for purposes of trade or commerce, in connection with mineral working, e.g. oil, bauxite, iron ore, or with the operations of large industrial plants (company towns). In Chapter 2, the nineteenth century 'ideal communities' and model villages were mentioned, as were the embodiment of the ideas of Ebenezer Howard in the private enterprise garden cities of Letchworth and Welwyn in the early twentieth century, to which later new towns, not only in Britain but also elsewhere in the world, owe so much.

However, in this country, New Towns — with capital letters — is the description usually applied to towns founded as a result of the New Towns Act of 1946, primarily as largely self-contained balanced communities of people and their employment with the object of relieving urban congestion in existing large cities and of preventing the further outward spread of such cities. Somewhat loosely, the term is also applied to existing towns greatly expanded on similar lines under the same Act.

Twelve New Towns were designated in the four years between 1946 and 1950. Not surprisingly, eight of these were around London where, following the Second World War, the need was very great. The famous Greater London Plan of 1944 had recommended a number of new 'satellite' towns and these New Towns implemented the proposal. Other New Towns were started in the Midlands, two in Scotland and one in South Wales. They were not constructed on wholly greenfield sites. There was usually an existing village or small town. Welwyn Garden City which to some extent had become a dormitory suburb of London was taken over, and one Midland town had really begun as a residential development for workers in a large steelworks located in that place for accessibility to raw material.

Nevertheless, the original purpose in all the early examples was primarily to take population and employment away from metropolitan areas. It was vital to provide local work of suitable kinds for as many of the inhabitants as possible or the towns would degenerate into well-laid out commuter suburbs. At first, the intention was to limit the size of New Towns to 50 000 people and to surround them by green belts, much as had been the basic plan for Letchworth and Welwyn, but these limits have been extended considerably. The structure of the Towns made use of the 'neighbourhood unit' concept, that is, a division into residential areas of about 8000 to 10 000 persons for whom it was estimated two primary schools would be required with an economic provision of shops, clinics, etc. The neighbourhoods are separated from one another by open space or school playing fields, and each neighbourhood has its own community centre for its residents. Each town has its main central area with public building and principal shops

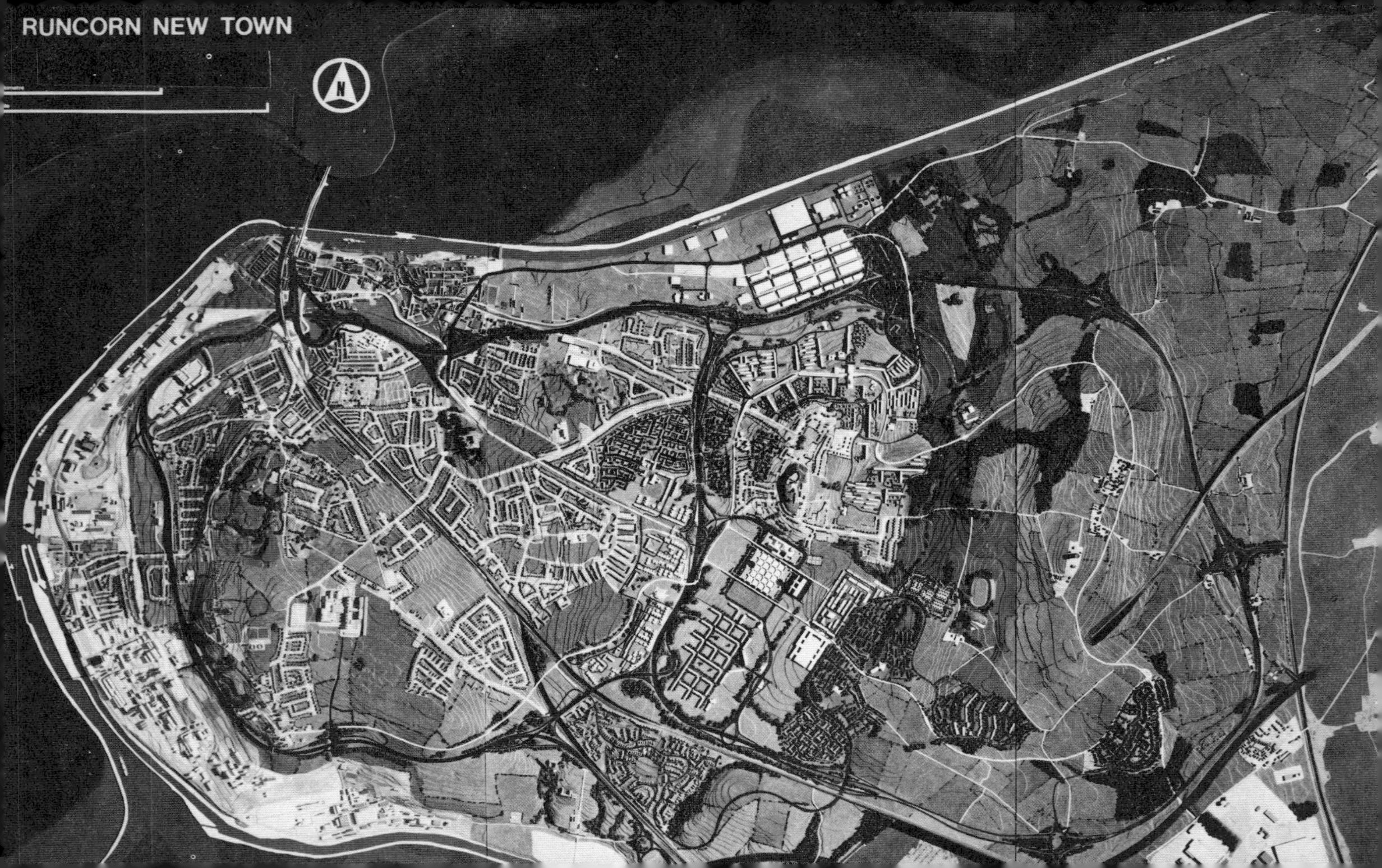
RUNCORN NEW TOWN

NEW TOWNS
Left: Scale model of Runcorn New Town, Cheshire, showing 'figure 8'
principal road system. Astmoor industrial estate – see picture on p. 80 –
to the north. *(photo: courtesy of Runcorn Development Corporation)*

Above: Aerial view of Cwmbran New Town, South Wales, showing town
centre with bus station, shops, offices and high-rise flats, and surrounding
residential areas. *(photo: courtesy of Cwmbran Development Corporation)*

NEW TOWNS INDUSTRIAL DEVELOPMENT   One of the main objects in the design of New Towns and expanded towns is the provision of employment opportunities in balance with residential accommodation. This often takes the form of industrial areas or estates. A striking example of the latter is the Astmoor estate — aerial view above — at Runcorn New Town where, in addition to laying out sites and roads, providing services and communications, the Development Corporation designed and built standard factories and landscaped open spaces. *(photo: Runcorn Development Corporation)*

Factory in landscaped surroundings, Washford Industrial Area, Redditch.
*(photo: reproduced by permission of Redditch Development Corporation)*

and major entertainment facilities, and there is one or more industrial areas. There was a recognition of the need to plan for motor traffic, to arrange for some degree of segregation of vehicles and pedestrians, and to provide a hierarchy of roads according to function. Since it was anticipated that the majority of the people attracted to the towns would be young married couples, emphasis was laid on the provision of family houses and gardens laid out so far as was economically possible in accordance with garden suburb ideals, which in many respects greatly influenced the design of the New Towns.

In due course, as is usually the case with any new development, the first batch of New Towns came in for criticism on a number of grounds. The neighbourhood concept was attacked on sociological grounds it being held that residential areas of such a size were too big for personal identification and did not engender community feeling or coherence. It was also said that separation of communities was contrary to the growing trend made possible by increased personal mobility in wider fields of social associations and interests. The distance between shops and primary schools was inconvenient for mothers of young children. Low density of housing, which was on conventional patterns reflecting traditional internal arrangements of rooms, was thought by

PUBLIC OPEN SPACE   The provision of open spaces for public enjoyment and play areas for children are considered essential elements in the design of residential areas.

Above is a picture of a youngsters play space close to Lumbertubs housing estate, Northampton. In the background is Billing Brook, alongside which is a pleasant walk forming part of an integrated system of footpaths linking amenity areas and dwellings. *(photo: courtesy Northampton Development Corporation)*

Below is seen a children's playground at Matchborough, Redditch New Town Worcestershire. *(photo: reproduced by permission of Redditch Development Corporation)*

some to be dull, and the general lack of compactness to cause a loss of 'urbanity' or affect the quality of a close and familiar environmental relationship. This was no doubt felt by some of the first inhabitants who had been used to the crowded conditions of big cities and had not become appreciative of compensating amenities, but less so by succeeding generations, especially as the towns became built up. There were some instances of over-provision of shops due to the impossibility of foreseeing at the time the effect of changing shopping habits resulting from the introduction of supermarkets and the greater use of private cars. The enormous increase in ownership of private cars was either not realised, or Treasury control on expenditure restricted adequate provision of private garages and parking spaces with a consequent congestion of residential roads in some parts caused by lines of stationary vehicles.

There was validity in some of the criticisms on the grounds of unsatisfactory programming, but others were made in the early stages of development when a proper balance between houses, factories and community facilities, and a balance in age structure had still to be achieved. Financial restraints in the initial developments had prevented the inclusion of major cultural and recreational buildings, and such desirable practical conveniences as district heating and cable television. However, as time has passed many of the shortcomings have been met, designs have been modified and with improvements in social life — the initiative for which must after all come from people themselves, the New Towns have shown that they are for many if not everyone very good places in which to live and work and their overall success is unquestionable. They are in fact considered the most successful outcome of post-war planning and they have inspired similar developments in other countries.

Nevertheless, as a result of the criticisms of the first phase of New Towns and the impact of new ideas, basic design principles were carefully reconsidered. In one direction, revised thinking was exemplified by the plans for the later New Towns of Cumbernauld and Skelmersdale which adopted higher densities of development and a generally more compact type of layout, bringing the central area within reasonable walking distance of most of the residential parts. Cumbernauld departed from the neighbourhood concept, provided a virtual complete segregation of vehicular and pedestrian traffic, and included a multi-level, multi-use town centre.

Subsequently, there was something of a return to the original New Town layout as its virtues became more apparent. But there were marked differences. The neighbourhood idea was based now upon a single two-form primary school with a closer relation to local shops and social facilities. Each residential area had physical identity of a differing character without spatial separation from other areas. The social units were smaller, of about 200 houses with corner shop and

play areas, the dwellings themselves formed into clusters around a semi-private open space, thereby providing smaller scales of environ-mental identification without inhibiting free inter-social movement. The town is regarded as a complex of overlapping structures. The designs of houses show radical changes in internal arrangement and are disposed in more imaginative layouts. Blocks of flats are used to a greater extent to provide the most satisfactory kind of dwelling for many categories of people e.g. active elderly, singles and childless couples, for whom houses and gardens are unsuitable.

At present, the establishment of completely new towns is less favoured than the expansion of existing towns – a proposed New Town for South Wales was disapproved in 1973 – either under the New Towns Act or the Town Development Act of 1952 (similar Act for Scotland 1957), under which finance became available to enable large cities to agree with small towns to accept their 'overspill' or excess population resulting from natural growth and lack of housing for those persons affected by slum clearance. The resultant development of the small towns is essentially of balanced residential and industrial design. Most town expansion schemes of this kind came about from straight arrangements between metropolitan cities and 'host' towns usually at the invitation of the latter without consideration of wider planning issues. But it was soon realised, partly from the findings of regional planning studies, that the relationship between town and town cannot be considered satisfactorily in isolation. There are issues arising from the relationship of an expanded town to its sub-region, and of groups of towns within a region. There are questions of deciding which towns should be encouraged to grow and to what extent.

And underlying these questions are fundamental issues common to New Towns and town expansions wherever they may be – issues that have to be continually re-examined in the light of central government policies, which are inevitably influenced by the international economic situation. Decisions in regard to location, limitations of size, regional factors, changing social mores, employment opportunities, traffic and communication problems, leisure and recreational requirements, and many more, are all of primary importance.

NEW TOWNS   Photograph of the central area of Tapiola Garden City, Espoo, Finland, about six miles from Helsinki. This fine example of a Continental new town, commenced 1953 by a Housing Foundation, was influenced in its planning by the ideas of Ebenezer Howard and the early British New Towns. Basically, it consists of three low-density neighbourhood units, each containing a mixture of houses and flats with local schools and shops, an industrial estate, and a town centre with multi-storey administration building, main shopping and commercial premises, cultural and recreational facilities, and principal church. The magnificent coastal site was well wooded, and almost all trees were preserved and integrated into extensive landscaping which is an important feature of the overall design. The town is a regional focus for a population of 80 000. *(photo: courtesy of the Museum of Finnish Architecture)*

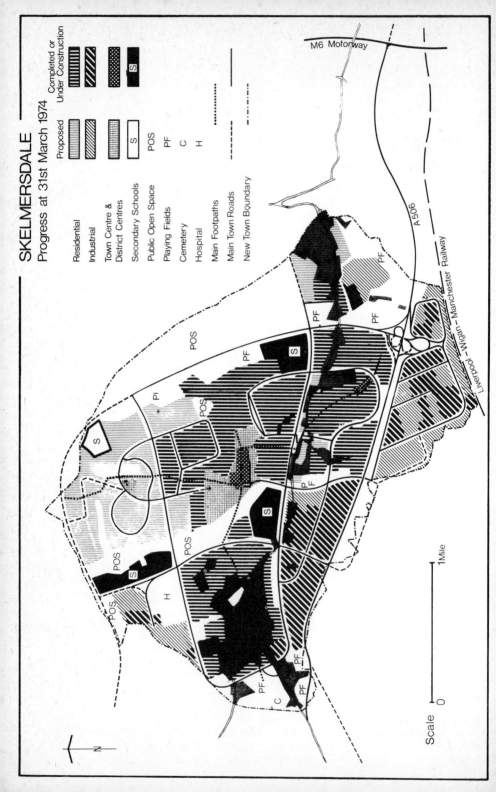

SKELMERSDALE
Progress at 31st March 1974

Completed or
Under Construction    Proposed

Residential

Industrial

Town Centre &
District Centres

Secondary Schools        S        S

Public Open Space                 POS

Playing Fields                     PF

Cemetery                           C

Hospital                           H

Main Footpaths

Main Town Roads

New Town Boundary

M6 Motorway

A 506

Liverpool – Wigan – Manchester Railway

Scale    0    1Mile

N

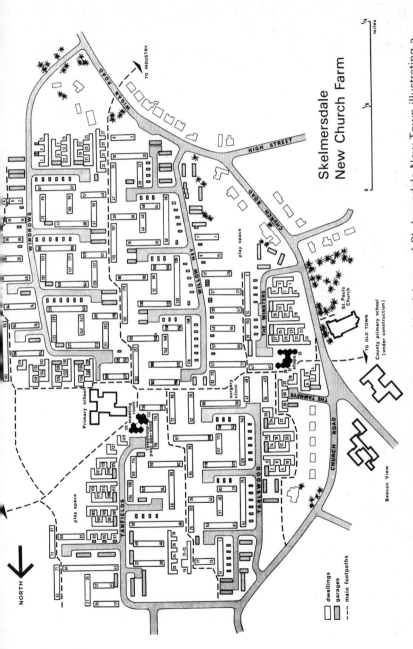

**RESIDENTIAL AREAS** Plan of New Church Farm residential area of Skelmersdale New Town illustrating a typical housing layout with local facilities distributed along the major footpath system, which also connects with the old town and county primary school, with the new town centre, and with the industrial area. *(plan: courtesy of Planning Director, Skelmersdale Development Corporation)*

NEW TOWN RESIDENTIAL AREAS   The residential developments of
New Towns are not efficiently laid out but the dwellings often reach a high
standard of architectural design combined with visual amenity. Two types
of housing at Redditch are illustrated. Top, houses with integral garages
built for sale by a private developer at Matchborough. Below, rented houses
in Lodge Park. *(photographs reproduced by permission of Redditch
Development Corporation)*

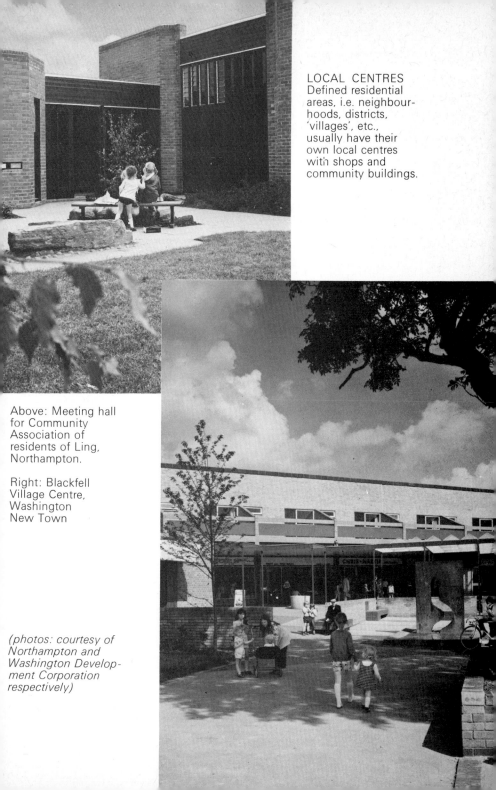

**LOCAL CENTRES**
Defined residential areas, i.e. neighbourhoods, districts, 'villages', etc., usually have their own local centres with shops and community buildings.

Above: Meeting hall for Community Association of residents of Ling, Northampton.

Right: Blackfell Village Centre, Washington New Town

*(photos: courtesy of Northampton and Washington Development Corporation respectively)*

**NEW TOWN COVERED SHOPPING CENTRE**   View from south-west of exterior of the Concourse Shopping Centre at Skelmersdale, Lancashire, with southern pedestrian access across cantilever footbridge; and a view of part of the interior on a busy shopping day. *(photos: courtesy of Planning Director, Skelmersdale Development Corporation)*

NEW TOWN MAJOR SHOPPING CENTRE BUILDINGS. Large central shopping buildings with adjoining car parks and designed for safe and convenient access on foot or by bus and car are a feature of many New Town developments.

The picture above shows the multi-storey car parks and busway in association with Runcorn's 'Shopping City'.

Below is an exterior view of Washington New Town's shopping centre 'The Galleries'.

*(photos: Runcorn and Washington Development Corporations respectively)*

COVERED SHOPPING CENTRES   A contrast between a nineteenth-century city centre shopping arcade, facing page, and a modern outer shopping centre: the 'County Arcade', Leeds, and the 'Arndale Centre', Crossgates. *(photos: courtesy of Director of Planning, Leeds City Council)*

## Rural planning

There is some difficulty in defining precisely rural areas because of the many encroachments on what was once open country and the various uses now put upon them. Negatively, it is land that in the main is not predominantly built-up, i.e. it is not manifestly urban. It is land that is a source of primary production and a source of materials, and which is the site of settlement, primarily in connection with agriculture, farming, forestry and cultivation, and with mining, quarrying and the working of minerals of all kinds. It is also the source of water supplies. But, at the same time, it remains a place for recreation where natural beauty of landscape, sea coasts, lakes and waterways may be enjoyed passively or actively. It is the habitat of animal and bird wild-life and of rare plants and flowers, and its rôle in the maintenance of ecological balance is important.

Its many uses are often in conflict with the natural environment and with one another. Because of developments that have already taken place and population pressures demanding more development and more space, carefully considered planning and control are essential. Decisions have to take into account competing and conflicting claims in the light of national policies, and with regard to resultant effects and interactions. Regional planning has to recognise all needs and provide a framework within which respective structure plans can be more specifically prepared. There are theories and techniques for evaluating uses and their effects, including anticipating future uses. Much legislation is directly concerned with rural aspects of planning. There are a number of societies and other bodies whose activities are aimed from different standpoints at the protection of rural land and life.

### Agriculture

One and perhaps the most important use of rural land is agriculture and farming. The growing of crops, rearing of sheep and cattle, etc., have been a part of country life since early times. Its importance has

RURAL RECREATION AND LEISURE   National Parks, see p. 99, afford varied opportunities for outdoor activities for millions of people every year, while retaining the practical uses of agriculture, forestry, water collection, etc. and remaining the habitat of wild life.
Left: an aerial view of Brecon Beacons, Wales. *(photo: West Air Photography)*

fluctuated in the past, but in the future it is likely to be highly important in Britain, since in the present overall economic climate the necessity to make the fullest productive use of every hectare of arable land is increasingly apparent. This situation will exert considerable constraint on urban development.

Agriculture is now industrialised and mechanised on a scientific and highly-capitalised basis, operated in part by syndicates whose management is organised for most profitable results. There can be conflict between the urgent need for rapid and efficient development on these lines and the protection of the ecological and visual qualities of the rural environment. The siting and design of various kinds of farm buildings, silos and other structures also give rise to concern.

## Forestry

Trees play an important part in maintaining ecological balance. They provide oxygen. They modify climate. They are necessary for certain species of wild-life. Once, Britain was largely covered by forests, but large-scale clearing for agriculture followed by the extensive use of indigenous timber for ship building and for the smelting of iron ore, has left little. Some of the existing forests were saved because they were royal hunting preserves.

Although the Royal Society of Arts encouraged landowners to plant five million trees in the eighteenth century, it was not until after the First World War that extensive reafforestation was started. The Forestry Commission, established in 1919, concentrated on the monoculture of fast-growing conifers and similar trees of greatest economic value but, in the opinion of many, not the most attractive of plantations. However, in recent years a greater variety of trees, including hardwoods, more suitable to different kinds of soil, have been introduced, and the Commission has also accepted the principle of multiple use, i.e. combining forest trails and creating forest parks.

Smaller clumps of trees and spinneys have for a long time been an ingredient of the beauty of Britain's landscape and they have practical value in giving shelter to wild-life. But they are threatened in some areas by modern farming methods, which are more efficient when applied to large cleared open ground, and in other instances by lack of money and skilled woodsmen to manage them after the break-up of big estates.

Above, right: one of the approach roads to the Lake District National Park. *(photo: Shaun Darley)*

NORTHUMBERLAND

NORTH YORK MOORS

LAKE DISTRICT

YORKSHIRE DALES

PEAK DISTRICT

SNOWDONIA

PEMBROKESHIRE
COAST

BRECON BEACONS

EXMOOR

DARTMOOR

CATIONS OF NATIONAL PARKS · ENGLAND & WALES

LEISURE AND RECREATION FACILITIES    Two photographs of Arrow Vally Park, Redditch New Town, Worcester, providing for all kinds of outdoor recreation, including a 28-acre man-made lake used for sailing, a golf course, and more than 100 acres of playing fields. The area between the lake and and the River Arrow, which has been realigned, is developed as a pleasant riverside walkway. *(photos: by courtesy of Redditch Development Corporation)*

Recreation and leisure

One of the most severe pressures on rural areas including the coast, and one which raises a number of issues in connection with preservation and conservation of the countryside, is that coming from the growing recreation and leisure needs of a large and increasing mobile affluent population. The situation is bound up with 'holidays with pay', car ownership, fewer workers needed because of automation, and the shorter working week. The 'three-day week' introduced at the time of the energy crisis in late 1973 may well become accepted as normal in some industries unless other considerations reverse the tendency to reduce the working hours.

Increased leisure in the rural context means amongst other things, a demand for the expansion of existing facilities, such as caravan and camping sites. But the provision of new facilities with all their attendant environmental problems, planning has to solve or at least mitigate.

Visitor accessibility to all places of natural beauty brings with it the threat of traffic congestion and undesirable obtrusive elements that tend to destroy the delights and benefits which are the basic attraction of the places. This applies particularly to National Parks which are now within easy reach of large numbers of people. It is estimated that fifteen million people are within a three-hour drive of a National Park. The Peak Park in the Midlands has twelve million visitors per annum. Some go to drive around or picnic, others to engage in countryside pursuits like walking and climbing. But this extensive tract, in addition to providing for public enjoyment, has the practical uses of agriculture, forestry, collection and storage of water, mineral working, as well as being the habitat of wild-life. The continuance of these uses and, in some cases particularly, those of recreation and leisure, exerts heavy pressure for their expansion and complicates the task of determining priorities amongst conflicting claims.

The Peak Park and the Lake District Park are run by joint planning boards which work to secure and maintain a balance between the needs of man and nature by carefully considered land management and the coordination of interests. 'Access agreements' are made with farmers and landowners to permit regulated public over their properties, but in some parts of the Peak Park through driving by private cars is prohibited and some completely traffic-free central areas are set apart for peace and tranquility. The planning boards lay out caravan and camping sites while promoting ways of enhancing the landscape. They cooperate with afforestation interests in achieving a mutually satisfactory policy for the siting and planting of trees.

Other National Parks are administered, apparently for local political reasons, by committees. This has been criticised on the grounds that

COAST PRESERVATION    Two photographs of Britain's unspoiled and now protected coast.

Above: White Park Bay, County Antrim, a mile of fine white sand and an area of great natural beauty and archeological interest owned by the National Trust. *(photo: J Allen Cash, by permission of the National Trust)*

To left: Part of Exmoor National Park between Porlock and Lynton. *(photo: West Air Photography)*

RECLAMATION   Upper picture shows what was a disused quarry and rubbish tip now transformed into landscaped ponds of high amenity value, lower picture, designed by Northampton's Department of Architecture and Planning. After clearance and cleaning of excavation and removal of dead trees, new planting was carried out and the banks were grassed. The bottoms of the pools are pebbled, which keeps the water fresh. Fish have been successfully introduced, and it is hoped that the area will become attractive to wild fowl. *(photo: courtesy of Northampton Development Corporation)*

such administration may be more likely to accede on purely economic ground to demands for unsatisfactory developments, and thus the preservation of the landscape, which was encouraged by the creation of National Parks, may be placed in jeopardy.

Designated 'Areas of Outstanding Natural Beauty' are similar in character to National Parks although smaller in extent. They are administered by local planning authorities which are responsible for protecting and improving landscape and for arranging for reasonable public access.

In addition to inland areas of relatively unspoiled natural beauty, there are stretches of coast of special scenic quality, which can also be designated, and thereafter planned and managed to protect them from unsightly building developments and the ravages of too much traffic and too many people. The National Trust and the Commons, Open Spaces and Footpaths Preservation Society are prominent in this kind of operation. The former has already acquired much of the coast, including in 1974 the 'white cliffs of Dover', and brought it under its aegis.

The Countryside Commission, see p. 62, is very much involved in all aspects of preservation and conservation for active and passive enjoyment. Another solution to the demand for open air leisure space, particularly for sports, is the creation of country parks specifically designed for various pursuits, and planned to accommodate large numbers of visitors. These have adequate and convenient access from centres of population, and so relieve pressure on National Parks and the countryside generally. As well as locations on upland and riverside valley sites, use can sometimes be made of derelict areas, e.g. by turning old quarries or excavations into boating lakes or otherwise reclaiming disused land.

There are more specialised reservations of scientific interest and these require to be more closely controlled and be made available only for serious study.

Reservoirs can be used for recreational purposes, e.g. fishing and yachting, provided that accessibility by road and parking facilities are sufficient for participants and spectators. The increasing use of water for recreation and sport — angling, skiing, speed boating, yachting and swimming — with their diverse space and seasonal requirements, is an important consideration in rural planning. Although there are calls for the allocation of more 'wilderness areas' where relative solitude in natural surroundings can be experienced, in general, rural areas for recreation must come under skilled multiple-use management which permits reasonable public access but which safeguards the preservation of natural and ecological conditions and the enhancement of essential

LANDSCAPING AND FACTORIES    The idea that industrial areas must be devoid of visual amenity is no longer acceptable. Two examples of factory buildings in combination with landscaping are illustrated: above — Pembo industrial estate, Skelmersdale, where use has been made of a natural water source with the addition of planting, and below — a manufacturing company's building at Welwyn Garden City with mature trees that are a feature of the town. (photos: courtesy of the Planning Director, Skelmersdale Development Corporation and the Commission for the New Towns respectively)

amenities. The problem is the realisation of this and the reconciliation of the conflicts of interests of the various sections of society.

## Industrial and similar uses

Although agriculture, farming and forestry, because of mechanisation and the methods of management now employed, can be classified as industries, there are more conventional industrial practices in rural areas.

Large-scale installations are being sited increasingly in the countryside. Some of them are thus located for ready access to the raw materials upon which they depend, e.g. clay, limestone, coal, and various kinds of metals, or where they are convenient for off-shore oil and gas production. These natural resources are of great importance to the national economy, and in some cases government departments are involved in their exploitation. Unfortunately, the extraction of minerals and other operations are seldom neat and tidy businesses. Such workings and industrial plants may be in conflict with the needs of agricultural development, and, because of their buildings and structures, associated heavy traffic, disposal of wastes and effluents, and possibly air pollution can be regarded as potential destroyers of scenic beauty. In consequence, conservationists and others who care deeply about the countryside are concerned about new proposals of this sort, which become planning issues that often have to be resolved by public inquiry. There are cases, however, where the central government may consider the work to be so urgently needed in the national interest that other considerations must be put aside.

Other kinds of industrial uses that raise similar issues are those connected with statutory undertakings, e.g. dams, reservoirs, hydro-electric and nuclear generating stations. Dams have a majestic beauty and can be designed to fit into their surroundings, but their location may have undesirable agricultural and social consequences. However, practical requirements, as with power stations, limit the choice of sites, and the demands for water and electricity for domestic and manufacturing purposes continue to increase and have to be met.

In general manufacturing industries, there is a long tradition of country locations, but most of the early mills disappeared with the coming of the industrial revolution and the concentration of factories in towns. However, nowadays some light industries are continued or permitted in rural areas. Those that are based on agricultural, farming or dairying operations or products are clearly suitable, provided siting, services and communications cause no problems. And small, in-offensive factories not tied to particular locations but which require low overheads and a good supply of labour, may well be of value in creating local employment opportunities, especially for women, if

POWER  STATIONS    Amongst large industrial developments in rural areas
are electricity generating stations with their attendant radiating transmission
lines and pylons, all of which can cause concern because of their effect
on the country scene. Nevertheless, as these examples show, such stations
can be sources of visual satisfaction by reason of their strong designs and
interesting forms and compositions.

care is taken to ensure that buildings and ancillary structures are not an intrusion into the rural scene.

Of a somewhat different nature, are the many installations and enormous quantities of land held by the Ministry of Defence, one of the largest single land administrators in the country. Many people feel that more of this land could be released and made available for at least recreation and holiday uses. But apart from defence needs, actual or potential, which would seem a not unreasonable argument in favour of retention by the armed forces, the areas concerned are said to be usually well-managed and maintained to the undoubted benefit of wild-life and natural vegetation, and so are helpful in preserving an ecological reserve that might be quickly destroyed by an invasion of campers, caravanners and holiday-makers generally! Also, at a number of establishments, medical and other services and community facilities are afforded civilian employees and their families from nearby settlements.

## Communications in rural areas

For some centuries the greater part of rural Britain has been covered by a close network of roads and railways and, to a lesser extent, canals and waterways, the original construction of which left much land neglected and derelict. The more recent advent of modern motorways and associated main roads and junctions have more seriously affected the countryside, and although care is now taken to avoid past mistakes and to mitigate adverse environmental effects, there are instances where the siting of new highways can become a matter of dispute between economic and engineering factors and considerations of landscape disturbance.

The siting of new airports or the expansion of existing airports is another planning issue that causes controversy amongst parties representing different interests. Large amounts of land are required not only for the operations of aircraft and their ground facilities, but also for peripheral developments such as the generation of traffic needed to move people and goods by surface transport to and from neighbouring towns. There is also the noise problem, still to be successfully tackled, which affects very wide areas.

The effect of electricity transmission by pylons and cables over the countryside is sufficiently well-known to require no more than a passing reference as another demand plus economics versus environmental conservation issue.

Above: coal-fired power station at Ratcliffe-on-sea, near Nottingham
*(photo: courtesy of Central Electricity Generating Board)*

Below: nuclear power station at Oldbury on the Severn Estuary *(photo: West Air Photography)*

Rural settlements

Since early times there have been and there still are many kinds of isolated dwellings in rural areas from 'stately homes' and mansions in extensive parklands to scattered farms and farm cottages on hill and dale. Regrettably, there are also many ill-designed and all too badly located houses and bungalows which, however much they delight their respective occupiers, are blots on the landscape. It is now practice, on grounds of amenity and because of the uneconomical provision of public services, not to permit such individual residences beyond the fringes of metropolitan areas or elsewhere in the countryside, unless there is very good reason for them, but to urge people wishing to live out of town to settle in those villages where additional development can be accepted.

Villages

Villages vary greatly in size and character. What is perhaps common to all is the absence of industry on any large scale — so-called mining villages are an exception — and the presence of at least one church, a public house, a shop and a primary school. They are more or less compact groups of buildings with probably a nucleus of older houses (important architecturally and historically), with possibly some inter-war council houses (often of unsympathetic materials and design) and more recent private developments. In most cases, villages were originally the focal points of agricultural or fishing communities, and they may still consist predominantly of the homes of those engaged in such work, even if the traditional social structures have been lost.

A lessening of the need for farm workers, and the lack of adequate public services and educational and social facilities have led to a general migration, especially by younger people, from country to town or to fresh fields overseas. There has been a concomitant decline in the agricultural village. On the other hand, the increase in personal mobility has brought incomers to some villages not too distant from towns, and the houses that were once the homes of country folk have been purchased and modernised to become high-priced properties for commuters, 'retireds' and week-enders, sometimes causing a shortage of suitable accommodation for young local inhabitants. The social, economic and physical consequences arising from these influxes of affluent citizens, and the pressures on more remote villages that have become attractive to tourists and seasonal holiday-makers are planning issues of some concern.

HYDRO-ELECTRIC GENERATING STATION, SCOTLAND   Aerial photograph of the dam on the shoulder of the mountain, the upper reservoir of the pump storage scheme at Cruachan in Argyll; below is the inlet/outlet of the power station which is actually located inside the mountain. *(photo: courtesy of North of Scotland Hydro-Electric Board)*

Picture above shows the so-called 'Spaghetti Junction' in Birmingham, a complex interchange in a built-up area. The construction of elevated motorways in close proximity to dwellings and other buildings with resultant problems of noise, vibration and atmospheric pollutants causes considerable concern. *(photo: West Air Photography)*

A three-level interchange between motorways M4 and M5 in more or less open country at Almondsbury, Gloucestershire. *(photo: West Air Photography)*

Planning policy for villages must be considered in the regional context with particular regard to social and economic factors, public transport and the capacity of public services. Villages are often considered as 'action areas'. But one of the first steps in considering any village is to determine if a need for development exists, e g. to meet natural growth, to satisfy an economic change such as might result from tourist development, or because of other outside pressures like the previously mentioned categories of commuters and part-time residents, as well as more general population trends.

Decisions have to be made as to which villages should be permitted or encouraged to grow, and which should have little or no expansion.

Matters that have to be considered in new developments include the avoidance of harm to the existing character of the village — an aspect of conservation — and to the surrounding countryside; views both into and from the village have to be taken into account. The possible effect on the social and cultural life must also be considered to ensure that this is not destroyed or disrupted. And, to get down to more practical aspects, regard has to be paid to the adequacy or economical extension of water, sewerage and electricity services. There will be traffic and transport problems to be solved: the diversion of through traffic, the provision of additional parking and perhaps of garages to older houses. More people mean more private cars, more services and delivery vehicles, and so, unless proper control is exercised, the possibility of traffic congestion and a threat to amenities is increased. The effects of growth on shopping facilities has to be studied. Underlying all these matters is the making of decisions in respect to the location and phasing of new residential and other buildings.

## Small country towns

In addition to villages there are, in predominantly rural areas, still some small towns of historical interest and visual charm, which away from the country's main growth areas have declined in population and prosperity, possibly owing to the loss of some of their marketing functions because of changed economic conditions. Their beauty and character should be preserved, but it might not be unreasonable to attempt to restore them to vigorous and vital life as regional sub-centres for service and social life for the surrounding area by carefully planning new developments integrated with the old, and thus attract additional population and industry as part of a balanced regional scheme.

## Ecology and pollution

Ecological considerations are often referred to in modern planning, so what is ecology? It is the scientific study of living organisms in relation to their surroundings or environment — which is not a bad definition of one aspect of planning! An ecological system or 'eco-system' as it is sometimes called, is one of a self sustaining community of plants or animals existing in its own particular environment.

The world contains many such systems, some of which are quite simple and limited in extent, but the world as a whole can be regarded as one great and complex ecological system in which man in relation to his environment is the dominant subject.

An important difference, however, between this conception and other ecosystems is that man, in contrast to other living organisms, has not only the ability to adapt himself to many different natural conditions, but can also change his environment and has enormous technological powers to do so. This, indeed, is what he has done and continues to do on an ever increasing and sometimes irresponsible scale in the construction of habitations and settlements, in creating towns, and in carrying out industrial operations and civil engineering works, including roads and other means of communication.

Life, in the final analysis, depends upon what are described as the fundamental processes by which carbon, nitrogen, oxygen, phosphorus and sulphur continually pass through the bodies of living things and back into the environment. These processes require the action of bacteria, which are essential for decomposition, and of single-cell plants which are the agents of primary production in the oceans. Anything that interferes with these fundamental processes in the biosphere may have repercussions of the gravest consequence on the physical well-being of human existence on this planet.

Clearly, then, planning in the broadest sense must be concerned with the critical situation that mis-use of the environment can cause, and as a first consideration must be directed by an understanding of and a desire to work with biological forces and not to ignore or go against them. In some instances this may need action at global level as, for example, control of atomic radiation or other major atmospheric pollutions; in other cases at international or national levels, but many are more or less local problems that can be dealt with within the scope of normal planning or particular legislation, e.g. the Clean Air Act.

In studying man's natural environment and, in particular, natural resources, it is essentially land, water and air and their derivatives in the physical sense, and space and amenity in the very real but less tangible sense, with which we are concerned.

It is in the exploitation of physical resources without proper planning and control that danger to the environment lies. Pressures on natural resources have built up because of the absence or inadequacy of planning and control in the past, to a state where the critical ecological capacity, which is the level of use beyond which the environment is adversely affected, is likely to be reached in the foreseeable future. These pressures have arisen from the explosive growth of populations in many parts of the world with, in most cases, an increase in spending power and leisure, thus causing ever-bigger demands for raw materials, water, food, energy, consumer goods, buildings, roads and recreational facilities and at the same time producing more and more waste and pollution.

To permit such pressures to go unchecked could lead to disaster. It is a function of planning, as an instrument of government policy, to ensure the good management of natural resources; that is, to organise and successfully use them, but with full regard to ecological factors. This includes the conservation, or husbanding and renewal, and perhaps the increasing use of those resources which can be so renewed or increased by man's agency. But there are some resources which are not renewable, such as the fossil fuels of coal and oil and natural gas and metals. These resources may well be completely exhausted before long and although the ecological effects may in these cases be relatively minor, there are other non-renewable resources, e.g. forests and topsoils, the disappearance or erosion of which could have serious consequences.

The pollution of rivers and seas by the discharge of toxic products from industrial processes or from ships and aircraft has been a subject of concern for some years, and efforts are being made to prohibit or limit such pollution along with the curtailment of the dumping of arsenic, copper, phosphorus compounds and zinc. A principle now being widely recognised is that the safe disposal of dangerous wastes should be the responsibility of those concerned with their production, and further that such products should be converted or utilised in some way, even when it is not strictly economical to do so, and should not merely be discarded to pollute or disfigure the environment. A recent idea is that industries should maintain a kind of information exchange which might facilitate the greater use by some industries of the 'waste products' of others.

Towns and their inhabitants may be regarded as ecological systems. Broadly, the analogy is that towns and conurbations exhibit in their organisation, patterns of arrangement and development and growth, decay and renewal, similar to those observed in some natural ecological systems. It would follow therefore that by an understanding of the basic causes of expansion, limitation and change, and by the way change generates further change, lesson valuable to the planning process can be learned. However, while there may be an element of truth in this, and unquestionably the systems framework idea owes much to ecological studies, it might be held that towns are subjected to influences beyond the range of natural systems. This is despite the use of sophisticated forecasting techniques, and the conditioning of human behaviour by its interaction with the environment.

PRESERVATION OF HISTORIC BUILDINGS 'Before' and 'After' photographs of a pair of eighteenth-century houses acquired by the Bath Preservation Trust when the building was threatened by demolition. The Trust restored the houses and sold the property subject to restrictive covenants which will preserve it from destruction or mutilation. *(reproduction by permission of the Bath Preservation Trust)*

## Urban preservation and conservation

Although planning is much concerned with future developments, it is also concerned with the preservation of existing buildings of architectural merit or historic interest, and with the conservation of urban areas of special character or visual quality. As noted in Chapter 3 legislation provides for this, and it is a function of planning authorities to implement the law.

Distress and regret at the destruction of fine old buildings to make way for new developments is largely a twentieth century attitude which has grown and become more widely accepted, parallel with the idea of planning and planning control. At the time of the first world war an essayist writing about demolition of some of London's historic buildings expressed his feelings in these words, 'While the huns are abroad in Belgium, the vandals are busy at home'! Similar feelings activated the formation of various societies whose object was the safeguarding of buildings of past periods. In due course, the spread of the preservationist idea and the appreciation that stronger action was needed than was possible within the limitations of voluntary organisations, led to the incorporation of protective measures in the Town and Country Planning Act of 1962, which introduced the concept of 'listed buildings' and made such buildings the subject of special control. This had the effect of bringing a great many individual buildings, some of comparatively humble origin, within the scope of legislative protection, but it did little to preserve the character or special visual quality, actual or potential, of historic urban areas. Further pressure by private organisations and influential persons resulted in the Civic Amenities Act of 1967 which empowered local planning authorities to designate areas, particularly town centres, of 'special architectural or historic interest the character or appearance of which it is desirable to preserve or enhance as 'conservation areas', and requiring that special attention be paid to such areas by planning authorities in exercising their planning and planning control functions. The foregoing legislation was included in the Town and Country Planning Acts of 1971 and 1972 and have been briefly described on pp. 47 and 48. However, at the time of writing, additional provisions are contemplated by the Town and Country Amenities Bill. The main provisions are:

i to enable local authorities to acquire compulsorily any listed building at existing use value as opposed to 'development value';
ii to enable the Secretary of State for the Environment to designate conservation areas in cases of failure or reluctance on the part of the local authority to do so;
iii to ensure that special publicity is given to planning applications

which, in the opinion of the authority, affect the setting of a listed building;

iv to require owners to pay when councils have to make emergency repairs to historic buildings.

It might appear that nowadays there is a general acceptance of the ideas of preservation and conservation, and that legislation is adequate for the achievement of their objectives. However, while there is usually no great difficulty in cases of buildings of distinction or areas of outstanding visual impact or strong historical association, in other words what may be classified as showplaces or tourist attractions, it is on properties and places of less obvious cultural or aesthetic values that differencies of opinion arise. The economic aspect becomes an issue. Sometimes this is seen as a conflict of interests between those members of the public with a personal liking for and a special knowledge of particular periods of art and history on the one hand, and commercial property developers and recalcitrant government agencies on the other. But such polarisation is not altogether incredible. There are many problems, and decisions are no more easy to arrive at than in other aspects of planning.

The attitude of property developers may seem clear enough. They are in business to provide accommodation to meet a market demand in a way that will give them a profit. It can be understood, if not forgiven, that this could lead to the demolition of decayed and despoiled eighteenth century houses which would be very costly to restore and rehabilitate for any modern use. Such work could be prohibitively uneconomical in ordinary terms. The new development might also lead to the erection of a multi-storey office building that could be environmentally disastrous to the surrounding areas. Nevertheless it could be argued that such commercial development was necessary to revitalise a run-down district or was an integral element of a larger redevelopment that would be in the real interests of the citizens at large, especially if land were thereby released for much-needed housing or recreational space as part of the package. Similarly, conservation as a principle may not receive entire public sympathy if its application would mean the retention of a row of picturesque but insanitary old cottages and thus prevent an industrial expansion that would provide more jobs for local workers in an area of high unemployment, or the keeping of decrepit Georgian terraces or Victorian mansions at the cost of inconveniently located shops, loss of local business opportunities and longer journeys to work. In these hypothetical instances it is possible, given time and expertise, that acceptable solutions could be found, but although the majority if not all local authorities accept their legal responsibilities in matters involving preservation and conservation, and would seek to resolve such situations satisfactorily, they have difficulties because of understaffing, especially the lack of suitably qualified staff, and in finding the money for acquisitions or other incidental expenses. Finance is also a source of difficulty in other cases, e.g. the carrying out of improvements to enhance conservation areas and of repairs and renovations to buildings to make them capable of continued use; and then there is the problem of finding suitable uses for retained buildings. Statutory protection does not make an unwanted building needed in the practical sense, except in times of exceptionally high property values.

In general, however, the economic aspects of preservation and conservation are intensified in periods of national economic stress. Not only are funds less readily available for such purposes, but the urgent need for maximum exploitation of sources of raw materials and energy and for the highest efficiency in the production and distribution of goods for overseas markets, i.e. improved communications, may over-ride considerations of less vital importance. While this may affect the countryside more than the older parts of towns, so firmly established are the principles of preservation and conservation in the minds of a large section of the public and many politicians that it is unlikely they will ever again be ignored as they once were, although in some circumstances compromises may have to be reached.

Nothwithstanding acceptance that preservation and conservation are desirable in certain cases, the criticism is sometimes advanced that some voluntary societies are over-zealous in their attitudes and activities. It has been suggested that the very words preservation and conservation imply a nostalgia for supposed ideal qualities of design, a looking back to visual scenes of delights of the past but ignoring changed or changing social conditions, a reactionary movement that is inimical to progress and real improvement in the physical environment. The appeal of the past may well be in part the result of disenchantment with the present and doubts about the future of architecture and planning. This criticism is linked to the belief that voluntary societies, which are still the main motivating force in conservation, are non-representative of the community as a whole and that their attitudes are those of the upper and middle classes; the attitudes of people who are themselves comfortably housed and financially secure and who are prepared to see towns stagnate if needs be rather than have their cosy life-styles disturbed by change. These criticisms may be unfair, but they must be faced. Conservation issues must in all cases of doubt be objectively examined and carefully assessed.

## Visual aspect of planning

Concern for the social, economic and ecological components of planning, on which great emphasis is rightly placed at present, cannot overshadow the importance of the visual element in the physical implementation of planning proposals. Indeed, it would be detrimental to, if not destructive of, the full intentions of planning; if careful consideration were not given at all stages to the achievement of the best possible visual qualities, both for functional efficiency and general amenity, in all new designs and in the improvement and enhancement of existing urban and rural developments which, unplanned, decayed or neglected, are offensive to the eye. The appearance of our surroundings touches our lives in every respect, and there are few people who do not respond or react consciously or sub-consciously to what they see about them, quite apart from the practical needs of the moment.

The idea that the general public is only interested in the materialistic provisions of planning is not borne out by surveys of, for example, completed housing schemes which show that the average person is very much concerned with the visual amenities, or the lack of them, of the area where he lives. This applies also to the places where he works and where he seeks rest and recreation.

Evidence of the former is afforded by instances of difficulties experienced by industrial firms in recruiting workers for plants that consist unnecessarily of a chaotic jumble of dirty and squalid buildings, even though general conditions of employment are attractive in other respects.

Historically, a desire for good design, visual as well as practical, is illustrated by the orderly if primitive arrangements of many early settlements and the layouts of native huts, and by the highly organised planning of great periods of civilisation such as Classical Greek and Roman, the Renaissance and the Baroque, the eighteenth century in Britain, and the formal civic designs of the nineteenth and early twentieth centuries in the western world.

Today, the difference from previous times is that it is now a tenet of planning that concern for visual qualities should not be confined to a relatively few impressive set-pieces, but should apply equally to the whole built environment — residential, commercial, industrial, etc. — and to the whole coutryside. Everyone everywhere has a right to freedom from the ugly, the dull and the unsightly.

However, the recurrent problem that faces planners is the determination of what constitutes good visual design. The question is less easy to answer than it should be because of unrealistic ideas of the past but which continue to be propagated, and in which the word beauty and its derivatives tend to confuse the issue. What is or what is not beautiful in the visual sense is highly subjective and individual.

What is needed is an objective approach based upon design principles that meet with common agreement, and that will lead to an environment visually acceptable to the great majority.

In many respects this has already been achieved, and there is an increasing measure of agreement, together with a growing appreciation that the application of basic design principles is just as valid for physical planning as for any created object. Certainly, there are special considerations in the case of the environment, at which people do not merely stand and stare, but within which they move and perceive not only through sight but also by other sensory experiences under continually changing conditions, conditions which are moreover subject to influences beyond the designers' control. Nevertheless, these special considerations can be taken into account, and it is necessary for all concerned with planning to study and understand fundamental principles of visual and other kinds of perception, and to put aside personal prejudices and preferences in the interests of achieving the ultimate goal of an environment that is agreeable and satisfying. Those who are directly concerned with physical planning, i.e. urban designers, architects and landscape architects, need to become even more sensitive to the many factors involved, and more skilled in the application of design principles in the exercise of their respective creative specialisms.

While it is not a purpose of this book to discuss environmental design in detail,* the opportunity may be taken at least of removing the misconception that there is an element of mystique or that the act of designing is mainly intuitive.

The design process is a logical sequence of:
   i definition of objectives;
   ii collection and analysis of relevant information and data;
   iii synthesis to meet all requirement within the context of prevailing policies and constraints; and
   iv ultimate implementation.

Visual design is in fact, always a part of this total design and cannot be successfully divorced from the functional and structural. In other words, appearance should be an expression of purpose or use and of materials and methods of production.

From this essential foundation and the primary compositional need for integrity and unity, good visual design is achieved by the careful

---

* An introduction to the subject is contained in R. Fraser Reekie, *Design in the Built Environment*, Edward Arnold (1972).

selection and skilled manipulation of forms, shapes and lines, colours and textures, with due regard to the inter-relationship of building masses, and open and enclosed spaces.

## Practical achievement of good visual design

How good is environmental design to be achieved in practice? Early planning acts gave little guidance and that mostly of a negative nature. The 1947 Act was primarily concentrated on land-use allocation and was little concerned with design. Control was exercised as a rule of thumb. But under new planning legislation and with new attitudes the opportunity is presented for more positive advice yet without undue restriction of the freedom of designers of particular developments.

## Structure plans

The first stage of development plan procedure, the preparation of a Structure Plan, should *inter alia* include a clear statement setting out operational guidelines for new works on the one hand and for the preservation of what is good in existing urban and rural areas. In this connection vaguely expressed intentions are insufficient, and the desired ends must be capable of practical implementation.

In the formulation of the statement, it may well be appropriate in certain cases for the general public to be consulted. It is part of a planner's job to take account of the effect of alternative proposals on the public before whom they should be put in a way which can be understood. There is more than one public, and that ideas of what is visually acceptable or unacceptable will vary from one group of people to another, and it is too much to expect that truly objective opinions can always be obtained. A simple majority of views may not be the determining factor. But as people become better informed and more discriminating, and less influenced by fashion and imposed 'trends', their contribution can be most valuable. Participation in actual design situations is in itself educational for participants and planners alike.

DESIGN GUIDES   Some planning authorities have prepared or are preparing guides to provide frameworks within which intending developers can produce acceptable designs, see p. 124. The illustration to the right shows one of the most comprehensive of such guides, 'The Design Guide for Residential Areas', which includes sections on Physical and Visual Criteria, various Case Studies, and a valuable appendix on basic design theory. *(photo of cover and pages by author with permission of Essex County Council)*

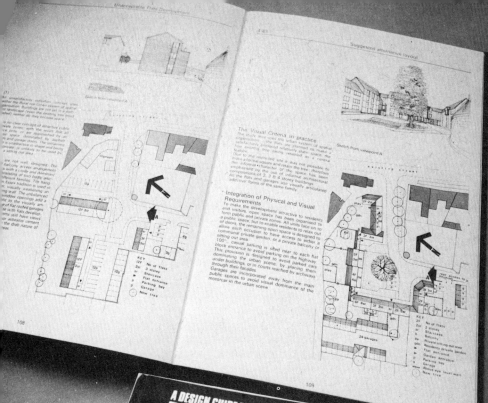

Switch from viewpoint A

EXISTING COURT

EXISTING COURT

### The Visual Criteria in practice

The study area uses the urban system of spatial organisation — the flats are planned to make the satisfactory enclosed relatively static space, the exciting free plains possible as a central feature.

Due to the restricted site it was not possible to make a spacious square and retain the tree, therefore the informal character of the space has been emphasised by the use of informal architectural compositions of 2, 3 & 4 storey buildings. All the flats and garages units visually articulated as additive forms of the same family.

### Integration of Physical and Visual Requirements

To make the development attractive to residents and visitors, open space has been organised to form public and private zones. All units face on to a public space, but to enable residents to relax out of doors, the remaining open space is designed to allow each occupier to have access to either a communal private garden, or a private balcony or sitting out area.

100° casual parking is sited near to each flat block entrance to avoid parking on the highway. This provision is designed to avoid parked cars dominating the urban scene, by placing them under buildings or in courts reached by archways through their facades.

Garages are incorporated away from the main public spaces to avoid visual dominance of the motorcar in the urban scene.

KEY
12F  No of flats
3s  2 storey
   Staircase
   Flat entrance
P  Parking bay
G  Garage
○  New tree

KEY
2F  No of flats
2st  2 storey
   Balcony
Hr  Mixed sitting out area
   Residents private garden
   Flat entrance
   Garden entrance
P  Parking bay
G  Garage
   Above eye level wall
○  New tree

108

109

# A DESIGN GUIDE FOR RESIDENTIAL AREAS

## COUNTY COUNCIL OF ESSEX

Local plans

Having established goals and criteria through structure plans, we use local plans to define design aims and objectives more specifically. These indicate areas of land use with greater precision by showing the general disposition of buildings and other structures, by directing the integration of townscape and landscape, and by setting out the relationship of new developments with existing developments, including conservation areas, and individual works of architectural, historic or archaeological merit.

The guidelines and briefs thus prepared provide architects and others with positive frameworks and references within which such professionals can produce their designs.

They are also employed for the better understanding of the possibilities of the physical realisation of local planning proposals by elected representatives, by other planning and local government officers, and by individual applicants* who may have little prior knowledge of the visual component in urban design or the rural scene.

In the preparation of local plans, the Local Authorities (District Authorities) should have capable urban designers, usually planner-architects, either as members of their staffs or specialist private consultants, and it has been suggested that there should be a register of urban designers, architects and landscape architects qualified and experienced in this kind of work.

The exercise of development control by planning authorities provides further opportunities for seeing that new private developments are carried out in accordance with the intentions of relevant structure, that local plans consider visual design, and that particular legislation in this connection is observed, e.g. tree preservation, siting of caravan parks, conservation of areas of special landscape or scientific interest, preservation of historic buildings, and control of advertisements. Reference may be made to local Architectural Advisory Panels in respect of building developments in certain instances or, in cases of national importance, to the Royal Fine Arts commission.

* In Britain only one out of every four planning applications is made with the benefit of qualified professional advice.

# 6
# Planning Education

The education of those people whose future careers are to be concerned with planning, whether in the theory or practice, is obviously of great importance, and since changes in the processes of planning must be reflected by and, ideally, foreseen and provided for in the framework of planning education, curricula and syllabuses and methods of teaching are continually under discussion and revision.

In consequence, while many institutes of further and higher education offer an increasing range of courses for the many different types of planners that are required by the complexities of modern life, there is, at any time, a variety in emphasis and content.

However, the common objective is to produce people who are equipped with adequate knowledge, appropriate skills, and with economic and social awareness to enable them to work effectively and pursue worthwhile careers, whether in the service of central or local government planning agencies, or in private planning consultancy, or in one of the specialised related fields.

Typical course objectives of a school of planning are as follows:
Subject Objectives

> An ability to comprehend the process of thought and procedure of problem identification, problem solving, optimisation and management in the planning process.

> An ability to appreciate the moral and political values and philosophical assumptions inherent in planning.

> An ability to consider the economic, political, social, aesthetic, technological and ecological aspects of the environmental system.

> An ability to understand the special distribution of human activities

125

and the linkages between them.

An ability to use skills and techniques in analysing and monitoring the environmental system.

An ability to appreciate the various constraints and inhibitions which limit the realisation of planning goals.

An ability to communicate and discuss planning problems with colleagues, other professional groups, elected representatives of the people, and with the public.

Education Objectives

An education which seeks to stimulate and develop the various cognitive skills of comprehension and analysis, synthesis and evaluation, which encourages both logical and creative thought processes.

An education which seeks to stimulate and develop the various effective skills of receiving, responding, and value organisation.

An education which seeks to stimulate and develop the various psycho-motor skills involved in articulating and presenting ideas and facts.

To create an environment which encourages a constant and continuing questioning of assumptions and beliefs.

An education which provides a developing appreciation of the complex implications of planning.

An education which encourages students to develop their own interest and specialisms within the general field of planning.

An education which encourages students to learn by doing things themselves whilst under the guidance of staff.

To create an environment which is conducive to the free communication of ideas, criticisms, and comment between staff and students.

Societal Objectives

An education which seeks to meet the demand for professional qualified planners.

But to create a course which is not exclusively vocational, but which is sufficiently broad to equip graduates to perform other rôles in society.

An education which encourages planners to respond to the needs, values and attitudes of different groups in society.

An education which will promote communication with the public and so stimulate public participation in planning.

To involve both staff and students in planning issues and problems.

There are at present between sixty and seventy general planning courses in Britain, mainly at universities and polytechnics, for both undergraduate and graduate students to enable them to qualify for careers in the profession.

Undergraduate education for students, who usually start direct from secondary schools and who must have at least five GCE passes including two at 'A' level, generally consists of four years full-time academic study or, in some cases, of a five years 'sandwich' course which includes a year of practical experience.

For those who have already qualified in some related discipline such as architecture, geography, sociology, or economics, there are two year full-time or three year part-time courses. Most part-time students are working in planning offices.

The generally recognised qualification for planners in Britain has been and is likely to remain, notwithstanding some differences of opinion, membership of the Royal Town Planning Institute (RTPI). At present, membership is obtained by passing the Institute's own examinations or the examinations of 'recognised' schools, and by complying with the additional requirement of two years' practical experience. However, in August 1973 the Institute published a discussion paper on changes in education and membership policy. It acknowledged that it is no longer possible for every planner to be an expert in every aspect of planning, and that the Institute's examinations as originally devised are no longer appropriate and should be phased out. They would be replaced by undergraduate and graduate courses at schools of planning, which would be free individually to innovate and experiment and perhaps become centres of excellence in particular aspects. Courses for students unable to attend such schools might be provided by the Open University.

The discussion paper suggested that planning schools could provide a combination of 'Foundation' courses and 'Applied' courses. 'Foundation' courses would deal with the broad principles of planning and the knowledge and range of skills required for a professional career; in the 'Applied' course emphasis would be laid on a particular field or subject area of planning, and on the application of the foundation studies to that particular aspect.

It is considered that this modular arrangement would allow the planning educational system to grow, develop and respond to changes in the scope and practice of planning as they occur. There would be a number of educational routes to qualification for membership of the Institute, but the essential object would be that a member by training and experience would be adequately equipped to discharge professional planning responsibilities effectively, whether they be of a generalised or specialised nature.

Related courses

Apart from professional courses in such subjects as architecture, landscape design, surveying in its several branches, and civil engineering, all of which involve to some extent the study of planning, there are a number of courses offered regularly by Universities, polytechnics and other institutes dealing with particular aspects.

Some of these may be specialist courses of one year or two years duration leading to a diploma or a degree. Examples are courses in regional planning, urban design, and transport planning. There are courses devoted to rural resource planning and to urban renewal and redevelopment, to name but two, and when the nuermous courses based on sociology and economics are taken into account along with courses designed to meet the needs of development in the areas of 'emergent nations', the list is a long and growing one. Educational institutions endeavour to keep pace with changing requirements not only in regard to planning practice but also as regards new ideas in theory and technology.

### Mid-career and short courses

Primarily, these courses which cover periods of a few days, are for practising planners to improve their expertise and help bring them up-to-date in concepts and techniques that have emerged in recent years. They also provide opportunities for post-qualification specialisations. The RTPI encourages such refresher courses, and the Department of the Environment and the Welsh Office sponsor mid-career training courses particularly aimed at planning officers affected by local government reorganisation.

In general, subjects are numerous and may include data management systems, process modelling, community action and local government, corporate policy planning, and so on.

Courses organised on similar lines, but on a broader basis provide opportunities for laymen as well as professionals both to learn from experts and to discuss perennial problems such as housing standards, pollution, or current topics arising from planning proposals affecting a particular locality.

### Open University courses

Although the Open University does not, at the time of writing, offer courses specifically in town and country planning, its Faculty of Social Science includes a course in urban development primarily from the sociological angle and contains introductory elements of environmental studies.

In the future, if the RTPI's own examinations are phased out it is likely that the needs of undergraduate students unable to attend normal professional courses will be met by the Open University.

The Open University may also provide in cooperation with established planning schools, a course for post-graduate qualification.

## Technicians' courses

There is a recognised and defined category of workers in planning offices whose function is to support their professional colleagues by carrying out essential activities particularly in regard to information gathering and processing techniques, and in the presentation of ideas and proposals by the methods referred to in Chapter 4, but the formulation of policy and decision making are not their concerns.

These Planning Technicians, as they are called, can acquire an academic qualification by taking special courses which have been established in a number of technical colleges and some polytechnics throughout the country. Normally, students are employed by planning authorities who release them for periodic attendance at classes, usually held for two full consecutive days every two weeks. The original syllabuses were prepared by a Joint Committee for National Certificates in Surveying, Cartography and Planning, but the responsible body is now the Technicians Education Council (TEC).

General education entry requirements are lower than those for professional courses, being four GCE level passes including mathematics and a subject involving a facility in written English. Examinations for the Ordinary National Certificate (ONC) are taken at the end of the second year of the course, and for the Higher National Certificate (HNC) at the end of the fourth year. These certificates may be superseded by TEC awards of comparable standards at some future date.

While it is possible for a suitable planning technician to proceed to professional training after obtaining the HNC, this method is not regarded at present as a general avenue of entry to professional qualification.

## Environmental studies in secondary schools

In recent years, environmental studies, particularly with regard to ecological and human geographical aspects, have been introduced into secondary schools' curricula, with examinations at GCE 'O' level. It is likely that these studies will be extended to 'A' level in the near future and will cover other fields such as physical environmental planning aspects.

The recognition of the importance of a basic understanding of planning problems in general education has been a special concern of the Town and Country Planning Association, which formed an environmental education unit in 1971 to help foster interest and give practical assistance. The unit works in close cooperation with official and other organisations, and members of the unit address meetings, conferences and classes in schools and colleges. Study sheets for classroom use have been published, and material to help teachers of environmental subjects is specially prepared from time to time.

A monthly Bulletin of Environmental Education (BEE) is of great value in teacher training, and the Association has also sponsored the Council for Urban Study Centres to provide residential and day courses with the object of informing teachers and children about the environment.

# 7
# Postscript

The intention of this postscript was to refer to any major changes in legislation or practice that might occur during the period from the completion of the draft text to the correction of proofs.

No such changes in basic legislation have been made, although it is expected that Government will proceed with legislation for the takeover of development land in accordance with a White Paper published in September 1974. It is not clear at present how the proposals will work out in practice.

There has been a multitude of modifications, variations in emphasis, guidelines and new proposals in a number of minor instances, some of which had been foreseen, and although there will doubtless be many more before publication, the essential content of the book is not nor will be thereby invalidated.

The book is not a handbook of current events in the field of planning but, as explained in the Preface, it is a work providing a background against which an understanding of what is happening can be facilitated and further studies of the diverse aspects of the subject can be made.

The opportunity may be taken, however, of summarising the situation as it exists. Primarily, today, planning is societal in its goals, that is, whatever the short term objectives and effects, the ultimate purpose is to produce and ensure a safer, healthier and pleasanter environment in which all people can live full lives. This involves economic considerations, the utilisation and conservation of resources, investment and financial management, and related overall strategies in a world context. These are the concern of governmental policies, from which it follows that planning must operate within a framework of law.

Ideally, and especially at a time of national and international crisis, cooperation will promote positive results whereas confrontation of opposing interests can only retard progress. Hopeful signs in this respect in regard to the aims of planning, as in other matters, is the apparent growing public awareness about the dangers of rigidly-held narrow sectional and ideological views including those of so-called pressure groups, and an appreciation that despite mistakes, difficulties and delays, much has been and is being done to improve the quality of life for everyone.

# Index

133